Leading Change

Olu Ajayi

- Fast track route to leading change in a fast-moving business world

- Covers the key areas of change leadership, from collaborative leadership to relationship management and from efficiency and efficacy to getting organizations ready for change

- Examples and lessons from some of the world's most successful businesses, including Microsoft, Daewoo, Cisco, The Royal/Dutch Shell, Komatsu, and ideas from the smartest thinkers, including Alan Hooper and John Kotter, Jeanie Daniel Duck, John Katzenbach and the RCL team, Daryl Conner, John Adair and Tom Peters

- Includes a glossary of key concepts and a comprehensive resources guide.

LEADING

08.06

>>EXPRESS EXEC.COM<<
essential management thinking at your fingertips

C000143957

First published 2002 by
Capstone Publishing (a Wiley company)
8 Newtec Place
Magdalen Road
Oxford OX4 1RE
United Kingdom
http://www.capstoneideas.com

CIP catalogue records for this book are available from the British Library and the US Library of Congress

ISBN 1-84112-205-X

Printed and bound in Great Britain

This book is printed on acid-free paper

Substantial discounts on bulk quantities of Capstone books are available to corporations, professional associations and other organizations. Please contact Capstone for more details on +44 (0)1865 798 623 or (fax) +44 (0)1865 240 941 or (e-mail) info@wiley-capstone.co.uk

Contents

Introduction to ExpressExec

ExpressExec is 3 million words of the latest management thinking compiled into 10 modules. Each module contains 10 individual titles forming a comprehensive resource of current business practice written by leading practitioners in their field. From brand management to balanced scorecard, ExpressExec enables you to grasp the key concepts behind each subject and implement the theory immediately. Each of the 100 titles is available in print and electronic formats.

Through the ExpressExec.com Website you will discover that you can access the complete resource in a number of ways:

» printed books or e-books;
» e-content – PDF or XML (for licensed syndication) adding value to an intranet or Internet site;
» a corporate e-learning/knowledge management solution providing a cost-effective platform for developing skills and sharing knowledge within an organization;
» bespoke delivery – tailored solutions to solve your need.

Why not visit www.expressexec.com and register for free key management briefings, a monthly newsletter and interactive skills checklists. Share your ideas about ExpressExec and your thoughts about business today.

Please contact elound@wiley-capstone.co.uk for more information.

Introduction To Leading Change

An introduction to the book and current themes on leadership and change.

"We're on the verge of all things new."

Billy Joel

The major exercise of our time is to envision and implement changes that generate dramatically better levels of performance at all levels. Continuous growth depends on it; everyone from the shareholder to employees, to customers is demanding it . . . and the change leaders are held accountable for it.

Some of the issues that the leaders in the twenty-first century face include: customer satisfaction; managing change; managing diversity; developing information technology and optimizing the use of the Internet; motivating core staff (intellectual assets) in a knowledge economy; and globalization.

The face of organizations has changed dramatically. As organizations, nations, and individuals have progressed, worthy notions of leadership have changed and evolved. Within organizations, structures are flatter, staff are more mobile, working patterns have changed; and power and authority are vested in the person, not in the position. In the words of US management guru, Steve Covey: "It is a white water world," and it is the job of leaders to embrace the chaos; lead dynamically; and to navigate the inevitable turbulence and change. The philosophy of leadership is not an unchanging monolith – as organizations evolve the philosophy of change is becoming more diverse and dynamic. What this means is that the basic truths will stay the same but they will always be subject to examinations and reinterpretation as time passes, and as the world moves on.

As this challenge becomes a daily reality, questions are being asked in quest of the *Holy Grail*. What is change? What is leadership? Why is leadership so challenging? What are the differentiating factors between change management and change leadership? What makes an inspired and inspiring leader? The answers can only be found as we immerse ourselves in the struggle and the experience.

In the words of Field Marshall Bill Slim (former governor general of Australia):

"the leader and those who follow him represent one of the oldest, most natural and most effective of human relationships."[1]

There is new emergent thinking on leadership as organizations and individuals seek today and tomorrow's leaders. As organizations are seeking to creatively inform and invent their futures, leadership development has become a critical issue.

In the middle of the swamp, a new breed of leaders is emerging and they are making a difference. This new breed is distinguished because they know that before they can implement meaningful and sustainable change, they must be willing to develop and change themselves. They must learn new skills and approaches for inspiring people; for influencing the behavior of people in a way that improves the health of the organization and that generates continuous improved results for the customers.

We can no longer discuss leadership in general terms. The approach to leading change must be situational. The underpinning of the *situational approach* is that it is the situation which determines who emerges as the leader and what style of leadership he or she has to adopt. Whether you are a CEO; a program director; a director of finance; a sales and marketing director; or an employee – your job is *change*.

Therefore this book will not seek to address leadership in a general sense, but will discuss leadership in the context of change and transformation. The approach in this book, therefore, is to conceptualize major transformations of organizations in terms of linkages between the content of change and its context and process; and to address the central ingredient of leadership behavior, in a complex, analytical, political, emotional, and cultural process of challenging the core beliefs, structure, and strategy of the organization.

This book will look at the evolution of leadership (with a strong emphasis on *change*), and explore the offerings of the legacy. It will explore and present the new emergent thinking on leadership and the differentiating factors of leadership. The book will look at how inspiring leaders have adapted to change and at key leadership characteristics.

I have done my best to write a book that is plain-speaking by eliminating a lot of consulting jargon that casts a veil and makes the do-able complex.

No doubt your organizations are experiencing waves of changes. I am certain that the greatest and the most effective organizations of change will be those that are led by real change leaders. A lot of organizations are beginning to realize this and are beginning to invest in building the capability and the competency needed for the mastery of change. This book deserves to be read by executives who have little time to sift for the nuggets in the dust of the bewildering jargon of *consultantese*. This is a book that is filled with substance and it is for those who wish to build and develop their skills to drive sustainable and fundamental change into their organizations and beyond; and for those who are seeking to find leaders and to develop leaders.

NOTES

1 Sharman, C. (1997) "Looking for tomorrow's leaders." *Management Today*, August.

Leading Change Today

What does leading change mean and demand today? What are the definitions of change and leadership? What are the lessons from old theories that twenty-first century leaders need to cherish?

"A man ran up to the Mullah, all joyful and excited. 'Mullah,' he cried, 'My daughter just got her MBA, she has finished all her learning.' The Mullah replied: 'I am sure God in his infinite mercy will give her some more.' "

Change is nothing new to leaders or to their organizations. Around 500BC, the Greek philosopher Heraclitus noted that: "you cannot step twice into the same river, for other waters are continually flowing on." He was one of the first Western philosophers to address the idea that the universe is in a constant state of flux.

As we move further from the "stable state," effective change leadership has become a challenging calling. However, like Peter Senge, I find it difficult to come up with a perfect definition for "change." This is because today, in the language of business, organizations, academia, and consultancy, the word "change" has come to mean different things to different people. We need to define "change leadership" in a way that establishes a congruence between leadership and the benefits of the change being implemented; and articulate it properly. Hopefully, I can then be like the NASA scientist, who when asked: "What do you do?" replied: "I help to put people on the moon." Such transparency, such congruence.

Change can refer to any of the following and more:

» external changes in the market/industry, technology, customers, competitors, social, political and natural environment;
» internal changes that determine how the organization reacts and adapts to the external changes at great speed;
» top-down programs such as business process re-engineering, restructuring, cultural change, for example; and
» business transformation programs which can be described as comprehensive organizational change initiatives, such as those at General Electric and Shell Oil;

It can also be a combination of all of the above.

My approach in this book is to treat "change" as meaning "major change." For this reason, I choose to adopt the definition of "major change" by John Katzenbach and the *Real Change Leaders* team:

"Major change is those situations in which corporate performance requires most people throughout the organization to learn new behaviors and skills. These new skills must add up to a competitive advantage for the enterprise, allowing it to produce better and better performance in shorter and shorter time frames."[1]

Change leadership can be defined as alerting groups to the need for changes in the way things are done; mobilizing and energizing groups; and tapping fully into the potential and the capacity of the organisation. It involves taking the responsibility to champion the change initiative and effort through building and maintaining commitment and support.

A good definition – but I think the answer is yet to be known. Change leadership is . . .? We will never cease from exploration. As George Benson said, we have to live life with an eraser.

There is a proliferation of literature on *leadership*; hence my angle in this book is to examine the leadership of change through the holistic study of actual behavior rather than in the scientific method of breaking the activities of change leaders and the responses of followers into categories of independent and dependent variables. Therefore, I shall concentrate more on what a change leader's activities are in leading and sustaining change processes, and less on leadership characteristics. The situation determines who emerges as the leader and what style of leadership he or she has to adopt. The situation will also determine the core skills needed to lead in that particular situation. Therefore, one can no longer discuss leadership in general terms.

For example, the leader and the style of leadership required in a stable organization will differ from that which is required in an organization under threat. This is because leadership styles and behaviors are likely to be critical in times of threats. In wartime, military leadership styles that emphasize dimensions of decisiveness and management control, are valued both in and out of the armed forces.

Therefore, the qualities, characteristics, and skills required in a leader are determined to a large extent by the demands of the situation in which he or she is to function as a leader.

At this point it is important to define *leadership* in this context. I do not seek to perpetuate the myth of the CEO as super hero as the perpetual change leader. In any major change program, there are many leaders because *there are many people at many levels in the hierarchy who play* **different** *critical roles during the change process, including the CEO.* In modern, complex organizations, the notion of an all-seeing, all-knowing leader is unrealistic. Instead, different individuals assume leadership in situations where they have a unique competence or accountability. All the non-CEO change leaders are every bit as essential to creating high-performing organizations as are the more visible and dynamic executive leaders. In essence, the change leader could be the CEO, a line leader, internal network, or a change community. It is very important to know that a sponsor (one of today's new words) and a change leader are not usually one and the same. I have worked on a number of change programs where the attitude of the sponsor has ranged from carte blanche confidence (that is, complete confidence in the program and approach) to lack of interest (that is, merely being involved with the program will avoid embarrassment).

Successful leaders of change tend to share a set of common characteristics. John Katzenbach and the RCL Team identified the following.

1 **Commitment to a better way**: they share an inexhaustible and visible commitment to a better way, continuous innovation. They also believe that the company's future depends upon the change – particularly their part of it – being successfully executed.

2 **Courage to challenge existing power bases and norms**: they develop the personal courage and resilience needed to sustain their commitment in the face of resistance and opposition. They are risk takers who learn to master fear, and thus inspire others around them.

3 **Personal initiative to go beyond defined boundaries**: they are not afraid to challenge the status quo and they consistently take the initiative to work with others to clear the drains and to solve problems. They do not wait for inspiration to find them, they are pro-active and they test and stretch the boundaries.

4 **Motivation of themselves and others**: they are inspired and inspiring leaders. They motivate others by creating a "can do" environment that is filled with excitement and momentum. They take personal responsibility for changing themselves and others around them. They are role models and they "walk the talk."

5 **Caring about how people are treated and enabled to perform**: they care about people and they are interested in developing others and enabling them to optimize their performance.

6 **Staying undercover**: they attribute part of their effectiveness to keeping a low profile and getting the job done.

7 **A sense of humor about themselves and their situations**: this helps them during the tough times. It helps them to stay the course in the face of confusion, discouragement and the inevitable failures that change produces.

I add:

8 **They are visionaries**: they create and live powerful persuasive visions that carry people along with them.

9 **They have an ability to skillfully read the situations they are attempting to change**: they are able to read the situations with various scenarios in mind and to forge actions that seem appropriate to the understandings thus obtained.

10 **They are lifelong learners**: they keep abreast of developments and they actively seek out development opportunities and experience. Learning gives breadth of perspective and understanding, and this ability to see the bigger picture and the opportunities it presents is a prerequisite for leadership vision.

11 **They are very good at building effective teams**: great leadership is dependent on great teamwork. This is highly important these days where we have a new type of team that is more fluid, flexible and virtual.

12 **They are open to challenge and to be challenged**: they ask questions, invite feedback, and they are open to be questioned. Asking for feedback at an individual, team and corporate level is essential to leading change and to maintaining and improving performance.

13 **They are men and women of courage**: real change leaders are not wallys. They have a firmness of mind and will face a difficult situation and they are willing to take risks and sometimes large gambles.

In his book, *Effective Leadership*, John Adair lists similar characteristics and their functional values.[2]

In 1999 Jack Welch, former CEO of General Electric, refined his views on leadership by creating a framework that wraps up leadership ingredients in four definitions: **E**nergy, **E**nergizer, **E**dge, and **E**xecution.

Whoever they are, leaders today all have to strive to gain and sustain a competitive edge. Bill Gates of Microsoft said he continually worries about competition. "In this business, by the time you realize you are in trouble, it's too late to save yourself," he said. "*Unless you are running all the time, you're gone.*"

There is a parable that expresses the same thought.

"Every morning in Africa when the sun comes up, a gazelle awakens and knows that it must run faster than the fastest lion, or it will perish. Every morning in Africa when the sun comes up, a lion awakens and knows that it must run faster than the slowest gazelle, or it will go hungry. It does not make any difference if you are a gazelle or a lion. Every morning in Africa when the sun comes up, you had better be running."

It is the law of the jungle. The business world has become a jungle and *"business as usual"* is a *"running game."* However, it is not just about running, it is about choosing to run; planning the run; being equipped to run; and winning the race. This requires innovation and mastery. In the words of Publilius: "anyone can hold the helm when the sea is calm."

It is a well-known fact now that organizational or business change cannot be endlessly "led" by replicating yesterday's practices to achieve success. Business conditions change and yesterday's assumptions and practices no longer work – this means that leadership of change must also change. There must be innovation (new ways of thinking and new lenses), and innovation means change.

SUMMARY

Anyone who has led a change program, successfully or not, knows that change is not a logical, linear, emotionless, and intellectual process. It is essentially an emotional proposition and there is no denying that old saying, *"no pain, no gain."* A change leader can have all the best laid plans in the world, but that is only the beginning. The change leader needs:

» a superhuman determination to make the change happen;
» persistence;
» stamina;
» a sufficient mandate that stems from personal change; and
» first-rate intelligence.

What then is the purpose of change leadership? In a nutshell, it is about building and sustaining a people-centric vision; leading the investment in the change effort; the management of time, energy and resources; and defining the purpose of leadership. Defining the purpose of leadership is even more important when there are several or more leaders within the organization. It is widely accepted these days that there is usually more than one leader within an organization. The growing complexity of business in a world of rapid change, globalization and technology assures that this is the case. It is the role of the change leader to ensure that all the leaders are aligned and engaged with a shared purpose.

Ultimately, leading change is not about "Star Trekking" and ordering the Trekkies to make it so. In the words of Tom Peters:

"Loosening the reins and allowing a thousand flowers to bloom is the best way to sustain vigour in perilous, gyrating times."[3]

And yes, it is still a jungle out there!

NOTES

1 Katzenbach J., Beckett, F., Dichter, S., Feigen, M., Gagnon, C., Hope, Q. & Ling, T. (1997) *Real Change Leaders*. Nicholas Brealey Publishing, London.
2 Adair, John (1983) *Effective Leadership*. Gower Press, London. pp. 55–57.
3 Peters, T. & Waterman Jr, R.H. (1982) *In Search of Excellence*. Harper and Row, London and New York.

The Evolution of Change Leadership

Evolution of leadership. A short history of the journey and of the *"here and now"* of leading change. A review of the legacy of past and present admired notions of leadership.

"Observe always that everything is the result of change, and get used to thinking there is nothing Nature loves so well as to change existing forms and to make new ones like them."

Marcus Aurelius (Roman Emperon)

In a state of stability, it is easy to believe that individuals in leadership positions make all the difference. But beyond the stable state, qualifications are being attached to "leadership" (hence, change leadership); questions are being raised about the potency of leaders in an ever-changing world, and the what, why, and how of translating noble aspirations into realized, sustainable change.

Over the last two decades, an era of rapid economic, social and organizational change, a number of writers have been exploring the relationship between leadership and change.

The list of the contributors to this recent research includes Warren Bennis (1989); Rosabeth Moss Kanter (1983, 1989); Alan Hooper and John Potter (1997, 2000); Peter Senge (1990, 1999); Daryl Conner (1994, 1998); John Kotter (1990); Charles Handy (1985, 1990, 1994); Bob Garratt (1994); John Adair (1983, 1989, 1998); Tom Peters and Robert Waterman (1982, 1997); Philip Sadler (1997); Bernard Bass (1990); Jon Katzenbach (1993, 1996, 1998); Peter Drucker (1955); Fred Fielder *et al.* (1976); Philip Sadler (1997); and Ken Blanchard and Paul Hershey (1969). This is by no means a complete list. The likes of Vroom and Yetton and style theorists such as Likert, McGregor, Blake and Mouton have also contributed greatly to this subject of leadership.

Over centuries, different theories of leadership have emerged. It is no surprise that the first theory to emerge after the Second World War was the Great Man approach to leadership (this approach has also been described as the Qualities approach or the Traits approach). This view of leadership regards the possession of particular qualities as the main reason why certain individuals are able to lead, guide, inspire, and direct others. This is a popular theory among philosophers and historians, and it has often been used as a justification for elitism within the society – for example Hitler's view of Germany being the master race and the British public school system. Although the military world has created a number of powerful leaders, it is increasingly acknowledged that the requirements for effective leadership in the armed forces are different from those in, for example, a small family firm.

One of the criticisms of this approach is that it takes no account of the context in which the leader operates, and it tells us nothing about what leaders actually do differently to followers. Another problem with this approach is that it makes it difficult to develop leaders, since it made the production of a definitive list of leadership qualities a dilemma. There are still followers of this theory today, many of whom believe that leaders are born and not made.

When the limitations of the Great Man approach were realized, theorists developed an alternative approach in the 1950s. The Style approach came at the time of reaction against scientific management and it represented a more democratic, humanistic approach. The Style approach to leadership pays greater attention to the style or manner of leaders' behavior towards their followers. The significance of this approach is that it concentrates on leadership activities rather than on leadership qualities. This approach draws attention to the fact that leadership is essentially an *activity*. It also expresses the view that leadership is concerned with people as well as with achieving end results. Hence the basic dimensions of "concern for people" and "concern for task." This approach to leadership still largely dominates managers' thinking today but it does not resolve the question of what makes an effective leader. The influence of this approach has been positive but it is flawed because it can, in my own understanding, be better understood and applied on a cultural basis rather than on an efficiency criterion.

The Style theorists include McGregor, Blake and Mouton.

The Situational Life Cycle Theory, developed by Hersey and Blanchard (1988), looked at the appropriate mix of task and relationship behaviors operating in the leadership situation. This approach centered on the idea that it was knowledge and appropriateness to the situation that defined the effectiveness of the leader. The criticism of this approach was that it placed too much emphasis on rigidity rather than on rigor. It implied that a leader may be effective in one situation, but not in another. In my opinion, the key is for leaders to develop their personality construct in order to sufficiently and appropriately cope in a number of different situations.

If the Situational approach were to be taken to the extreme, it would be a folly for an organization to let the *fates take the sole rein*, by allowing the situation or organizational dilemma determine who should be the leader.

In the 1960s Fred Fielder developed the Contingency Model of Leadership. This was one of the first leader-situation models to be developed and it was based on studies of a wide range of group situations. It also concentrated on the relationship between leadership and organizational performance. This development was significant because it highlighted a long-realized reality, namely that a leader needs to take account of the situation in which he or she is operating in order to decide on the appropriate style to adopt. In addition, the approach focused on the ability of the leader to handle the situation.

Contingency theories of leadership are underpinned by the belief that there is not a single style of leadership that is appropriate to all situations and that flexibility of style appropriate to the situation is the key. The major contingency models include:

» favourability of leadership situation (Fiedler);
» quality and acceptance of leader's decision (Vroom and Yetton, and Vroom and Jago);
» path-goal theory (House, and House and Dessler); and
» maturity of followers (Hershey and Blanchard, and Nicholls).

In the 1960s, John Adair, while advising on leadership training at Sandhurst military academy, developed a leadership model to identify the requirements for leadership. This model drew on the work of MacGregor, Maslow and Hertzberg and resulted in three overlapping areas of needs – those of the **Task**, the **Team**, and the **Individual** (see Fig. 3.1).

His *functional approach* to leadership draws upon the *qualities approach* but it applies the three circles to all those qualities in order to pick out all the essential ones and to determine when it is appropriate or not to demonstrate certain characteristics. This work is known as The Three Circles and it has proved to be a robust and enduring model in the UK. I believe that the beauty of this work by Adair was that first, it split the "people" element into two parts – that of the individual and

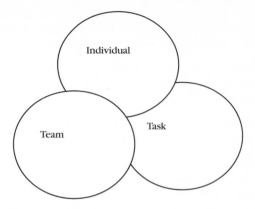

Fig. 3.1   The Three Circles.

that of the team – and second, it paved the way for the concept of leadership development.

The Best Fit approach was developed and promoted by the likes of Tannenbaum, Schmidt, George and Von der Embse, and it was an attempt to make the interactive nature of the three circles (or variables) more operational.

In 1985, Michael Welling, in his book *Behaviour Technology*, provided an alternative strategy for looking at issues of leadership in place of the traditional methods available. His work was concerned with improving business performance through a scientific approach to people issues and is underpinned by the frameworks of Transactional Analysis and the Problem Solving Dimensions. It proposes that:

> "behaviour technology provides a platform for the practising manager to understand the behaviour of subordinates and the task behaviours required."[1]

The last 20 years has also seen a shift from management to leadership, as a result of the recognition of the need to manage change, in particular the human elements of change. This has generated discussions on the distinctions between managers and leaders. This shift is based on the belief (linked to the Great Man approach) that leaders are born and not made. Drucker (writing originally in 1955) is quoted as saying that:

> "Leadership is of utmost importance. Indeed there is no substitute for it. But leadership cannot be created or promoted. It cannot be taught or learned."[2]

Field Marshall Bill Slim drew an interesting distinction between managers and leaders:

> "Leadership is of the spirit, compounded of personality and vision; its presence is an art. Management is of the mind, more a matter of accounts calculation, of statistics, of methods, timetables and routines: its practice is a science. Managers are necessary, leaders are essential. A good system will produce efficient managers, but more than that is needed. We must find managers who are not only skilled organizers, but who are also inspired and inspiring leaders."[3]

However, despite years of research studies into the common traits of leadership and studies by the likes of Byrd and Jennings, it has not been possible to determine one personality trait or set of qualities that distinguishes a leader from a non-leader. Although the role of the manager and that of the leader are synonymous, it would be an error to assume that every leader is a manager and vice versa. This erroneous assumption, which has been made time and time again, at a costly price, led to the conception of *The Peter Principle* (to promote one beyond his or her level of competency).

To illustrate the distinction between managers and leaders, C.M. Watson applied the differences to the 7-S organization framework of: strategy, structure, systems, style, staff, skills, and shared goals. Peters, Waterman, Pascale, and Athos developed this framework. Watson suggests that managers tend to rely on the "hard" Ss:

» strategy: the plan of action, which allows an organization to allocate its resources in order to get from a current state to a future (desired) state;

» structure: the way the clusters fit together; and
» systems: the way information is gathered, disseminated and assessed;

whereas leaders were inclined to rely on the "soft" Ss:

» style: the culture of the organization and the personality constructs and behaviors of the people that work for the organization;
» staff: the kinds of people that work the organization;
» skills: the differentiating competencies of the organization; and
» shared goals: the sets of values, beliefs, identity, principles, and priorities that characterize the organization.

With caution, Watson suggests that the 7-S management framework could be the domain of leaders. He suggests that managers may not ordinarily be capable of mastering all the 7-S to attain a consistently high level of organizational performance.

I believe that some people are born natural leaders but this is also shaped by nature, circumstances, culture and opportunities. I believe that there are some managers who have the potential to become leaders with the benefits of robust leadership development processes and coaching. There are also leaders who have had leadership thrust upon them because they were such good managers – usually this results in the loss of a good manager and the acquisition of a bad leader. Despite the differences, there is no denying the fact that there is a close relationship between leadership and management and it can be difficult to segregate them as distinct activities or two sides of the same coin.

In 1978, a book by James McGregor Burns kicked off the movement from Transactional Leadership to Transformational Leadership, and the movement from the Arnold Schwazenegger "command and control" style to that of "empowerment." In his book *Leadership*, Philip Sadler draws a succinct distinction between the two philosophies of leadership:

> "Transactional Leadership occurs when managers take the initiative in offering some form of need satisfaction in return for something valued by employees, such as pay. Transformational Leadership, however, is the process of engaging the commitment of employees in the context of shared vision."[4]

Table 3.1 A framework for the study of managerial leadership (adapted from the work of Laurie J Mullins in his book, *Management and Organisational Behaviour*).[5]

Approach	Period
Qualities or Traits approach (the "Great Man") Assumes leaders are born and not made. Leadership consists of certain inherited characteristics or personality traits. Focuses attention on the person in the job and not on the job itself.	Post-Second World War
The Functional or Group approach Attention is focused on the functions and responsibilities of leadership, what the leader actually does and the nature of the group. Assumes leadership skills can be learned and developed.	Early 1970s. Made popular by the works of Ralph Stogdill and John Adair
Leadership as a behavioral category The kinds of behavior of people in leadership positions and the influence on group performance. Draws attention to range of possible managerial behavior and importance of leadership style.	Early 1980s. Made popular by the work of Tannenbaum and Schmidt
The Styles approach The way in which the functions of leadership are carried out and the behavior adopted by managers towards subordinate staff. Concerned with the effects of leadership on those being led.	Made popular by the works of McGregor Blake and Mouton and supported by the work of Likert
The Contingency Theory This theory concentrated on the context of leadership activity. It focuses primarily on the ability of the leader to handle that context.	This research was kicked off by the work of Fielder in 1969, and carried on through the 1970s

Table 3.1 is a framework for the study of managerial leadership. Chapter 5 of this book will focus on the key issues today and current debate on the subject of leading change.

Table 3.1 *continued.*

Approach	Period
The Situational approach	
The importance of the situation. Interactions between the variables involved in the leadership situation and patterns of behavior. Belief that there is no single style of leadership appropriate to all situations.	1988. Featured the work of Hersey and Blanchard
Transformational Leadership approach	
A move from "command and control" to "empowerment" of the workforce. A process of engaging the commitment of employees in the context of shared vision, shared values and shared goals.	1990. Featured the work of Bernard Bass
The Learning Organization approach	
The focus is on the art and practice of the learning organizations and how leaders can develop effective learning organizations.	1990. Featured the work of Peter Senge
The Composite approach	
This is an approach that recognizes that effective leadership is not learned from a book or by studying and adhering to one particular leadership model.	1980s to present time

SUMMARY

As we sincerely seek to understand more about leadership, in particular about leading change in this most unstable state, the well quoted observation by T.S. Eliot springs to mind again and again:

"We must not cease from exploration and the end of all our exploring will be to arrive where we began and to know the place for the first time."[6]

The challenge that faces those that lead change these days is greater than ever due to the speed and the changing nature of change on both an organizational and a personal level. This calls for a more democratic, flexible and holistic approach. The leaders of change today will have to pay more attention to the *human* aspects of change and people are the main actors in the sphere of intellectual capital. Thank God for technology! But in addition to technology, the future is about people, communications, building communities of practice, organizational learning, knowledge and information. The practicalities of these requirements will be addressed in the last chapter of this book.

NOTES

1 Welling, M. (1985) *Behaviour Technology*, pp. 113–122. Gower Publishing Company Ltd, England.
2 Drucker, P.F. (1989) *The Practice of Management*, p.56. Heinemann Professional.
3 Sharman, C. (1997) "Looking for tomorrow's leaders." *Management Today*, August.
4 Sadler, P. (1997) *Leadership*. Kogan Page, London.
5 Mullins, L. J. (1985) *Management and Organisational Behaviour*, 4th edn. Pitman Publishing, London.
6 Eliot, T.S. (1942) "Little Gidding" from *Four Quartets*. Faber and Faber, London.

The E-Dimension of Managing Change

The implications of technology and its role in shaping the definition and broadening the role of change leaders.

"The dissemination of information is one of the cornerstones of modern civilization."

John F. Budd

The jungle has been electrified! In addition to the pressure of dealing with the normal, "business as usual" operational problems and that of navigating change after change in an increasingly global economy, those leading change now have to create the time to explore all the options available to them to develop themselves and their organizations *electronically*. It is now a wired world and the most successful change leaders will be those who tap into the wires and maximize the currents for the benefits of their organizations.

The advent of the Net has changed the landscape of the business world forever. It has done this by providing access to global markets and increased access to individual buyers, allowing the creation and realization of innovative business models, and enabling a more convenient and cost-effective interaction channel for businesses and customers alike.

The electronic age has led to an amazing increase in customer expectations. Now customers expect businesses to work 24/7 (that is, 24 hours a day, seven days a week) to give them access to business information; they want instant service or they will go elsewhere; they want a hassles-free service and they demand the best possible service and value from your offerings. Then there is the Intranet. Your staff expect the same. They want instant access to organizational information; instant access to the just-in-time learning that will enable them to do their jobs and provide an excellent service to your customers; they want instant communications about your business strategy, the *how*, the *when*, the *what* and the *who*. What the Net and the whole "e" ethos has done is to create a sense of urgency to accomplish these goals, while at the same time creating great opportunities to take them to amazing heights.

As the Net rides on majestically to change the world, in the sphere of business it is reshaping the nature and the logic of competition; the nature of communication; the scope of innovation; the speed of change; and the nature of leadership. The effective and successful change leaders will be those who embrace the Net with a militant pursuit of efficiency and tap into the real power and potential of the

Net to transform their businesses and their organizations. In his book, *The Digital Economy*,[1] Don Tapscott defined the five levels of change caused by the Net as: the development of the effective individual; the development of the high-performance team; the development of the integrated organization; the extended enterprise – xtranets, SCM, CRM; and the inter-networked business – networked value chain.

"E" DEVELOPMENTS

The following is a summary of some of the "e" developments.

E-learning

Electronic learning is a revolutionary new approach to training and developing employees and it is driving a quantum change in the nature of corporate training. With e-learning, organizations now have the powerful potential to develop, deliver, manage and measure the impact of training internally and externally using one centralized system.

Internally, the benefits are that it enables mass customization of learning and is more personalized (role based) and *just-in-time*. Also, the learning content is scalable, easier to update and re-usable – saving organizations time and money.

But e-learning's role is not limited to the provision of training to employees; part of its role is also to educate suppliers so they can have *current and live* knowledge of your requirements in order to provide a better service. For example, the better the quality of the training provided internally, the better the quality of the knowledge your staff will be able to share with your suppliers, thus building a stronger, more efficient and sustainable relationship.

The Net also enables you to educate your customers about your products in a more effective, consistent and timely manner; to consolidate your relationships with your partners by building and managing an effective channel that delivers timely and consistent training to your partners wherever they are.

One of the organizations taking advantage of the Net in a big way is Scottish Power. In the spring of 2001, it piloted a three-month home-learning scheme as a platform to make learning widely available to its employees and to their families. The results of the evaluation of the pilot will determine the next steps forward.

Knowledge management

Both knowledge management and e-leaning focus on a similar role – that of getting information and knowledge to the right people at the right time. However, where e-learning has focused on delivering courses and testing performance, knowledge management is a systemic process of capturing, interpreting, recording, storing and delivering knowledge throughout the organization. It focuses on capturing the organizational knowledge that exists in employees' heads and sharing it throughout the organization. For example, a sales manager who has developed a highly successful sales blueprint could, by using simple tools, quickly create and deliver a virtual seminar to share his insight with sales teams globally.

E-HR

The Net is also changing the very essence of Human Relationship Management. A key area of the way in which the Net is revolutionizing human resources (HR) is the automation of processes such as timesheets and expenses. One also has to consider the select benefits programs; their virtual, paperless implementation takes away the administrative burden of employee compensation and gives the HR department an opportunity to transform an organization's relationship with employees by personalizing it. With the increasing globalization of business and flexible work patterns, the Net provides the platform from which a centralized resource can be accessed remotely at any time, anywhere. Electronic HR will have a crucial role in transforming the staff/employer relationship. It also offers a strategic tool to recruit and retain the right staff so as to make the business more competitive. This last point is becoming critical in a new economy that has a very mobile workforce. Imogen Daniels, a CIPD advisor on resourcing and recruitment, said: "Employers are using the Internet as part of a belt and braces approach to ensure they are not missing out on the right candidates – especially given the tight labor market."

Customer Relationship Management

Customer Relationship Management (CRM) is the process that allows different kinds of customer data – personality constructs, lifestyle, transaction records, geo-demographics and market research – to be transformed for both tactical and strategic use. The business goals of market expansion remain the same but the Net has created a sense of urgency to accomplish these goals, while at the same time creating great opportunities to take them to spectacular new levels. The leaders of the Net economy achieve astounding business success by leveraging the Net to:

» grow customer relationships;
» maximize customer level; and
» make it easy to do business and to monitor business performance

in ways that were not possible before. And what are these leaders doing? They are being very proactive; they are getting to know their customers in order to serve them better, capture new or previously unseen value and grow their relationships with the best customers. They are re-inventing their businesses – re-visiting their business strategies and resource allocation to meet evolving customer needs. They are evaluating, re-designing and automating customer-impacting processes to make it easy for the customer to do business and to improve the transparency of the speed and quality of transactions, while increasing the effectiveness and efficiencies of their customer-facing operations. They are building a complete picture of their customers and are sharing relevant portions of this knowledge across the value chain for coordinated delivery of customer value.

Business intelligence

Business intelligence systems are a range of new IT tools that lets the ordinary office workers and managers – rather than IT professionals – access their companies' databases. The use of business intelligence is rapidly extending to other areas of business including e-commerce. For example, websites generate gigabytes of data a day that describe every action made by every visitor to the site. No bricks-and-mortar retailer carries the same level of detail about how visitors browse the offerings, the routes they take and even where they abandon transactions.

Organizational communications

The Intranet has opened up creative approaches to communications within the organization. Goodbye to boring old paper memos! The

Intranet enables timely, useful, and crucial information to be circulated to staff at the touch of a button. It is now a wired, wired world.

Other e-developments

These include: e-banking; data warehousing; B2B (business to business); research and development; and marketing and competitor analysis and trends forecasting.

Every minute there will be something new that we can use the Net to do. Not all of them will be useful, but an idea is born every minute. There is no time in this book (neither is it the intention of this book) to dig deeply into the topic of the Net economy – Chapter 9 of this book contains a list of useful resources.

LEADING THE "E" EVOLUTION

Leaders have to create a culture where the Net is your organization's second nature and where data is a living fountain of knowledge, and not a reservoir.

The leaders who work with their staff to release an "e-culture," are those who inspire people with their vision and credibility, and the Net is a huge factor in enabling such leadership.

Statistics reveal that only five percent of e-enabling programs have reached the point of transforming businesses into integrated Web-enabled organizations. A practical and effective route to this transformation can be broken down into three phases.

» Phase one is when the Internet is used to build efficacy – that is using the Internet to make existing business practices more effective and efficient (for example, "e-procurement" as a means of improving the buying functionality).
» Phase two focuses on business integration and value. That is, how separate parts of the business can work together to create a supply chain of functionality that responds to customer demands quickly and easily.
» Phase three brings the first two phases together to create an agile and flexible business that has the capability to respond quickly to customer demands as efficiently and cost-effectively as before but with both business and client having a vested interest in one another's business success.

By the time every business has integrated the Internet and digital technology into its operations, e-business will become normal business. This is not going to happen overnight but Cisco, Microsoft and Intel are examples of companies for which the Net has become second nature. In spite of their current struggles, they are role models not just of how Net companies operate today, but of how all companies will operate tomorrow. Take a look at Microsoft.

CASE STUDY
A story from Missouri

Two years ago, Microsoft embarked on its own large-scale Customer Relationship Management (CRM) project. Code-named Missouri, it was designed to replace hundreds of solutions used in sales and marketing in different countries with just six systems that would be used globally. There were a number of reasons for the change according to Shaun Orpen, customer marketing director of Microsoft UK. "Our customers operate in an increasingly global world and we also wanted to improve customer satisfaction by ensuring that we respond appropriately. Global solutions meant that we can modify our business more quickly."

Microsoft's customers range from a consumer buying a single copy of *Flight Simulator* to a multinational company purchasing thousands of software licenses, and, says Orpen, the biggest challenge was meeting the variety of requirements. The aim is to create a "virtual relationship" with each customer, whether the contact is via the Web, telephone, mail or any other channel.

The strategy was to implement best-of-breed software solutions for each of the main application areas. An initial phase, covering functions such as human resource management, finance and logistics based on SAP software, was completed 18 months into the project, and a second phase for sales engagement, based on Siebel Sales Enterprise, is almost complete. Further phases will include seminar and event management and customer management. The company intends to have a globally managed data warehouse, reflecting the increasingly global nature of marketing campaigns.

Explains Orpen: "The most important benefit will be to improve our relationship with the customer and to ensure customer satisfaction. One of the challenges has been to get buy-in from all of Microsoft's people. We have worked hard to get people to see this as a value-added investment rather than a tax. This is always the challenge when deploying new processes and systems."

Making it happen

» Identify the customer-related processes and capabilities where the greatest gains are to be made.

» Ensure that CRM has a champion at board level who is familiar with the complexities involved in making the project a reality.

» Don't assume a ready-made solution will solve your problems.

» Think about how your processes can become more customer-focused.

» Encourage your employees to see the customer as an investment, not as a cost. Involve as many people across functions as possible.

» If you learn something useful about your customers then act upon it. Communicate all new intelligence to your team at once.

» CRM is all-encompassing across a business. A project contained within the silo of one department is doomed to failure. Start small but think big, and integrate your people and processes as you go.

LESSONS LEARNT FROM THE CASE STUDY AND TIPS

» Success often hinges on aspects of management commitment, such as whether those driving the change are prepared to commit time, and whether there are "interested" sponsors and teams in place. I use the word "interested" because I have worked on change projects on which the sponsor was detached from the project in every sense except for signing the checks. At Microsoft, there was a strong commitment at executive level for the change to work and this laid the foundation for success.

» Change leaders have got to involve all the stakeholders. The influence of stakeholder groups cannot be dismissed. Today we are seeing that the stakeholder groups are having an increasing influence on the decisions, values, beliefs, and leadership of organizations. Effective stakeholder management is more than telling the groups what you are going to do. It has a great deal to do with involving, influencing, moral leadership, social responsibility, and integrity.

» The change leaders at Microsoft knew that the Internet was not just about technology. It is a known fact that whilst technology makes things happen, it is people that make things work. It is a mind-set: a new way of working, of communicating, relating, sharing, etc. It is a matter of changing every aspect of how a company works both internally and externally. Transformation to a Net culture involves a dramatic shift in the ways people work so you have to win their hearts and minds.

» Leaders should not try to radically transform their business in one go! It is a fact that being successful at e-business is synonymous with responding faster to market changes and customer needs; reducing operating costs; and increasing co-operation with your key customers and trading partners. However, companies should not jump on to the bandwagon without looking where it is heading and how it is going to get there.

» Change leaders have to invest a lot of resources in training. Organizations that overlooked training are still counting their huge losses as they mop up disastrous e-enabling projects. People need to be skilled-up to work in the new e-enabled environment and the most effective training is backed up by some robust internal support mechanisms, and coaching.

» Pre-announce, Announce, Post-announce. It is the change leader's role to ensure that all stakeholders are given a reason for the change and what it means for the organization, its staff and its customers, in the short, medium and long term.

» Change leaders must ensure that they have the right structure and infrastructure to support the change process. In addition, and very importantly, they must carry out an audit of the organization in order to confirm that they have the internal capability to change. To jump in with eyes closed and hands tied is corporate suicide.

» Change leaders should find the right balance between their aims for dexterity and their aim for growth. The explosion of the Net in the 1990s has given businesses a new mandate to stop cutting costs, and start growing revenues. In this new millennium the mandate for the next phase of the Web is for companies to get more disciplined about growth and to become more focused on adaptation. It's no longer enough just to grow, companies have to grow better. It is the job of the change leaders to focus companies on their ability to maneuver and to change direction.

» It is essential that valid measures exist to steer this explosion of new business. It is imperative for leaders to establish metrics and processes by which to measure and monitor the success of e-business. Proven measures such as Return on Investment (ROI) and Economic Value-Added (EVA) should be applied where e-business is generating revenue. Also the impacts on the business (such as customer impact, market place impact and organizational impact) should be assessed. It is true that not all areas of e-business will generate revenue, but leaders can still try to evaluate its value or impact on specific change programs. To do this, leaders would have to be more innovative and creative about how they define and measure "impact."

» Finally, change leaders need to work with their people to build e-communities in order to optimize the value of the Net. This is a powerful and interesting idea that needs to be fully explored because it will be a way for organizations to better leverage their intellectual capital – particularly as more and more leaders are now recognizing the fatality of loss of corporate memory. For example, it is impossible for anyone to track what each individual in a company knows. Leaders should identify and put into place mechanisms and structures and promote a culture that enables the company to share what people know collectively and to build communities that collaborate and share knowledge, resources and information within dispersed, global organizations.

NOTES

1 Tapscott D. (1996) *The Digital Economy*. McGraw Hill, New York.

The Global Dimension

Globalization – opportunities and threats. Extending the role of leadership in an increasingly inter-dependent world.

Globalization has been described as: "the interconnectedness of capital, production, ideas, and cultures at an increasing pace."[1]

Effective change leaders need to sow, feed, and disseminate the seeds of strong *geographical management*. This is essential for diversity management and for developing dispersed responsiveness. This would enable the business to read situations – sense, analyze, and proactively respond to the needs of the global markets.

Effective change leaders also need to build *strong business management* with global product responsibilities and service delivery capability if they are to dominate markets and to achieve global efficiency and efficacy, and integration.

Finally, by building a *worldwide functional management*, a business can develop the capability to build and to transfer its core competencies – a capability vital to worldwide learning and skills transfer. Furthermore, there is the need for those leading the organizations to ensure that in a globalized economy, linguistics will become one of the core competencies and a factor in competitiveness. Thus the links between the functional managers will allow the company to accumulate specialized knowledge and skills and to apply them wherever they are required in the global operations. Functional management will then act as the repository of organizational learning and as the prime mover for the consolidation and circulation of learning within the business.

No doubt, a company's ability to take into account and act on these issues will determine its global organizational capability and leadership mentality. This is the critical point where the wheat is separated from the chaff.

The advent of the global organization and economy makes good commercial sense, but it does not simplify the role of those who are leading change. Instead of one workforce, one way of working, one culture, one set of best practices, one leader ..., there are now issues of alignment, of accommodation of differences, of management of diversity, and of synchronization, in order to present a global view to both internal and external customers. In addition, there are different sets of expectations to be managed. Increasing globalization of economies and markets is forcing companies to optimize efficiency, efficacy, responsiveness, and learning in their worldwide operations and business transactions.

Most forward-thinking businesses today realize that their markets need to expand in order for them to survive. Their products, markets, suppliers, customers, and indeed their people place them firmly in a web of global operations whose complexity far exceeds what they had been equipped to cope with and manage in the past. As a result, many change leaders recognize the need to globalize and harmonize, but they are often baffled by how to accomplish this and how to find a balance between building better and building faster. Consequently, they struggle to find a strategy for operating on a global basis.

Distance, time, culture, history, demographics all play an important part in globalization. One can just imagine a process in which teams on different times, with different cultures, different work cultures and different languages share a day's work with the location of the work moving between, even at best, permeable boundaries. Throw in other dimensions such as customers, costs, markets, technology, competition and the dilemma facing the change leader becomes a Herculean task!

The very act of addressing these complex dimensions of a global economy is difficult and complex under any circumstances; but the task is complicated even further when companies add in the consideration of competitiveness.

Faced with the task of building multiple, and often complex, strategic capabilities in organizations, what is a change leader to do?

In numerous organizations, debates such as the following, are ongoing.

» What are the merits of pursuing a strategy of national responsiveness as opposed to one based on global integration and synchronization?
» Should key assets and resources be centralized or decentralized?
» Should the evolution of the business lead to strong central control or should it lead to greater subsidiary autonomy?
» How do we, as a global company, respond to indigenous needs and demands? What matters to the local people? How can we create a win-win situation that does not have the word *exploitation* stamped on it?
» How do we advocate a global economy that is not perceived by the locals as an economic assault – one that does not rob people of their dignity, their customs, spirituality and traditions? This applies

especially in a geographical location where people do not measure wealth in terms of money.

» How do we respond to broad, emerging strategic demands and issues in a global economy without eroding the effectiveness of our current uni-dimensional capability?

» How do we achieve a balance between building faster and building better, internally and externally?

Culture does play a critical part in this process of globalization. As barriers are brought down around the world, a big issue is how to manage transnational organizations. There is a growing literature on the cultures of organization and globalization, so this book will not attempt to dig deep into that area. In a global economy of free trade, new issues are emerging that are challenging the leaders of global businesses. They find themselves facing a multiplication of their organizations' complexities and pertinent cultural issues. This brings to mind a question posed to me by a colleague recently. This is real life and it goes some way to illustrate one of the dilemmas faced in a transnational business operations context.

The summary of the message is this:

"Olu, if you have got a moment, I would like to pick your brains. There is an urgency to this, which is why I did not call you about it. How should a change leader handle this situation? An Internet-based charity company is using a software development company based in Bulgaria. The charity wants to have closer control of their costs and asked (after years of doing business together) the staff in Bulgaria to start submitting timesheets to the charity.

"The feedback from the managing director of the Bulgarian company who asked his staff to complete the timesheets was: 'They feel like I am asking them to kill their mothers!'"

"Are there any techniques the change leader (in this instance, a project manager based in the United Kingdom) can use to get these timesheets completed?"

As one who is continually exploring questions about the dilemmas of leading change within and without, I realized that this was one of the many questions that is bound to come up more and more often in an increasingly globalized business world. For me, this example highlights the critical importance of the awareness of cultural differences and environments in the process of globalization.

The following is a good example of globalization gone wrong.

CASE STUDY
Daewoo's global expansion strategy

A good example of leading change in the global economy is Daewoo. Daewoo focused on achieving economies of scale by targeting the East European markets for its overseas capacity expansion, as a way of overcoming its manufacturing cost disadvantage in the domestic market vis-à-vis its main competitor, Hyundai. This initial pattern of decisions was formed mostly by such determining factors as top management's commitment to specific strategic decisions and resources, both managerial and financial. Subsequently, it was altered or reinforced as Daewoo accumulated different learning experiences that were well managed.

Daewoo started its car business in 1978 after acquiring Saehan Motor, formerly known as Shinjin Motor, from the Korean Development Bank (KDB). Shinjin was a joint venture with GM until 1992. After the break-up with GM, Daewoo promoted a new slogan "Global Management," and pursued globalization. Daewoo's globalization history can be divided into three phases: domestic (1967–1976), export (1976–1988); and globalization (1988–present).

In 1994, faced with stiff competition from Hyundai, Daewoo sought other ways to gain a competitive edge and found globalization to be the ideal solution. In 1994, it acquired FSL and FSO in Poland, and Rodae Automobile in Romania. By 1997, Daewoo had globalized into nine countries where it was managing 11 manufacturing and 30 marketing subsidiaries. Daewoo's globalization was fast paced and was characterized by its dual approach: it concentrated on manufacturing in Eastern Europe and the Asia-Pacific, while it invested heavily in marketing in Western Europe.

In order to find out why Daewoo pursued its particular globalization strategy, it is useful to see inside the minds of the key decision-makers. The following is a quote from Daewoo president,

Taegu Kim (Annual Report and *Chosun Daily*, January 4, 1994). It attests what top managers at Daewoo believed had motivated the company's globalization:

> "This year, Daewoo Motor Company will globalize in earnest. We will concentrate all our effort on reaching a production capacity of two million cars per year. But we cannot achieve this level of scale by staying in the Korean market alone. Since it is dominated by Hyundai, which has already established huge capacity, the Korean domestic car market becomes more saturated in terms of manufacturing capacity and thus less attractive for further investment in the capacity. Therefore, it is critical to shift our attention to foreign markets for capacity increase ... We will acquire foreign manufacturing sites and continue plant construction projects ..."

Facing severe cost disadvantage and small market share, Daewoo had to expand its manufacturing capacity in order to acquire much-needed economies of scale. And it had to do it fast, so that it could accomplish its top management's will to be a viable global carmaker. Consequently, Daewoo expanded its manufacturing functions into less advanced countries, especially in Eastern Europe, quite expeditiously. Daewoo did not face serious obstacles during its fast capacity expansion because it was relatively easy for it to take control over the outdated car companies in a struggling Eastern Europe. Moreover, the global financial market was quite supportive of Daewoo.

As an initial determining factor, top management's will to globalize played a critical role in shaping Daewoo's globalization motivation and strategy in the long run. In late 1999, Daewoo went bankrupt mainly due to its debt-financed capacity expansion in Eastern Europe.

LESSONS LEARNT FROM THE CASE STUDY

Regarding globalization, the leader at Daewoo had clear objectives. Daewoo Motor's president was determined to achieve economies of scale fast by expanding the manufacturing capacity abroad. Also, from his quote, it is clear that the primary reason for the scale of the global capacity expansion was related to the competitive situation in the domestic market. At the very outset, Daewoo's top management decided to be an independent carmaker in the global market with its own brand name and during that process the company seldom encountered serious difficulty, reinforcing its propensity to expand its capacity in the region. In contrast, its main competitor, Hyundai, had learnt from its failure to expand in Canada and had adopted a more cautious approach to expanding its capacity overseas.

Daewoo had to rely heavily on debt financing for its capacity expansion because it did not benefit much from the fact that it belonged to a business group (*chaebol*). Unlike other *cheabol* groups such as Hyundai, Daewoo started as a garment trader and grew mainly as an international trading company. The automobile industry is much different from the "soft" industries – it requires a different set of skills, competencies and experiences on the leaders' part than that useful in "soft" industries. As a result, Daewoo did not have enough manpower and the organizational capability to manage the manufacturing capacity which was being expanded quite extensively in such a short period of time. This was one of the fatal mistakes made during the Daewoo globalization process.

Daewoo is now making a brave comeback and trying to remake itself.

Adapted from an article written by Bowon Kim and
Yoonseok Lee, in *Long Range Planning*.[2]

SUMMARY

"Ani ve'ata, neshane et ha'olam. You and I will change the world."

In a global economy, the critical factor that positions a business for success is collaboration. Developing relationships, building alliances and partnerships will become the most important area of corporate strategy. Collaboration is key to corporate growth and development, diversity management, and to the attraction and retention of first-class knowledge workers.

Also, global businesses cannot operate in isolation. The leaders of global businesses must be aware of the impact of globalization in the world in which they operate – in particular, the ethics of globalization; the rippling effects on the worlds beyond their worlds; and the impact of their business practices and development on the environment.

Professor Paul Kennedy of Yale University believes that: "humankind prospers from the creation of a level global economic playing field, and many societies also prosper, but there is a downside . . . that individuals, companies and other societies do not . . . If the pace of change and intensity of the challenge is too severe, the number of those unable to compete might, in certain parts of the world, be dangerously large and lead to a political and ideological backlash."

This has already been witnessed in the intentions of the anti-capitalist demonstrators and fuel protestors across the world. Rightly, they believe that organizations and governments are not paying enough attention to the risks and the costs of globalization.

It is therefore imperative for leaders of global businesses to build strategic alliances with local businesses and to invest in the local businesses in order to build a platform for *win-win* situations.

Effective leaders of change in the global arena have got to ensure through themselves (as leaders) and with their employees, that they build a platform for global effectiveness: the leaders have to be able to operate effectively in different cultures, to manage and relish cultural diversity. They have to be able to obtain both the benefits of localization and those from being part of a major corporation. They need to visit other *villages* – that is, they need to be able to work effectively in domains that are external to them, such as strategic alliances and joint ventures.

"A person who knows only his own village will not understand it: only by seeing what is familiar in the light of what is the norm elsewhere will we be enabled to think afresh about what we know too well." (source unknown)

By "locking into" one village, we may, without intending it, limit and inhibit the realization of our basic ideals and values; and our businesses may lose out on the richness that can emerge from engaging with different meanings and purposes for learning to be globally effective.

NOTES

1 Ralls, J. (1996) "Globalization – the profit and the pain." *International Fund Strategies*, June. Centaur Publications, London.
2 Bowon Kim and Yoonseok Lee (2001) *Long Range Planning*, June. The Strategic Planning Society, London.

The State of the Art in Leading Change

An exploration of key issues, new thinking and new perspectives on leadership and change.

"Progressiveness is looking forward intelligently, looking within critically, and moving on incessantly."

Waldo Pondray Warren

This chapter will focus on the key issues and current debates today on how to lead change. There is a growing interest in how to lead change, not surprisingly, with Enterprise Resource Management; globalization; customer relationship management; e-enabling; Net technology etc. on the agenda of businesses. Emergent ideas and concepts abound and the challenge for the change leader lies in determining what is appropriate and what works, and what will not work.

This is a good thing because we are constantly evolving and we constantly have to reassess our tools, techniques and methods for leading change in order to ensure that we are leading change appropriately and effectively. The concepts include organizational learning; complexity thinking; performance management; strategic management; the balanced score card; empowerment; grassroots leadership; action learning; situational leadership and other organizational change tools.

There are many debates about change leadership today and I will endeavor to capture the main debates. The more we think we understand what leadership is, the more we realize we are yet to arrive at a commonly understood and accepted definition for a title that has so many facets.

Will the real change leader please stand up?

The myth of the CEO as the sole leader of change in an organization is dissolving. This is not to say that a CEO cannot be the change leader in a given circumstance; but there can be non-executive leaders that emerge naturally, usually in unstable states, to make a profound impact on the business and drive the change. This then leads on to the question of what makes a leader.

Change leadership styles – how should one lead?

After the untimely demise of projects or (as is becoming prevalent today, the crash of businesses – Marconi is a good example as I write), it is common to hear questions being asked about the leadership in the organizations. This leads me to conclude that some leaders get trapped in inappropriate patterns of leadership, which they then replicate from project to project or from organization to organization, regardless of the context, with disastrous results.

EXHIBIT 1: JOHN AKERS AT IBM

When appointed as CEO in 1985 John Akers acknowledged the need to reposition IBM strategically. Between 1986 and 1990 he initiated a number of major "rounds of action" to re-orientate the company and enhance its responsiveness to changing markets. Yet in 1991 the company experienced its worst performance since the mid-1940s with revenues down by $5bn, and decreased market share in all major geographic areas. In 1992 the company lost $4.97bn, racking up in the fourth quarter the largest quarterly loss in US history. On January 26, 1993, pressure from shareholders resulted in Mr Akers' resignation as CEO.

What went wrong during this period at IBM? Akers commented in 1991 on the complacency of "some of our people." More fundamentally, it seems that senior management still clung to well tried, but by then obsolete strategic recipes. Once-successful patterns of thought or collective beliefs led to failure to interpret appropriately the signals of major changes in the external world and to develop effective ways of behaving within it.

The critical importance of effective stakeholder management

Stakeholder management is one of the key buzzwords of today. The influence of stakeholders is on the increase and the challenge for leaders of change is how to manage communication across stakeholder groups.

Increasingly, leaders are beginning to realize that the mission is impossible without commitment. The wise men and women are beginning to dig deeper into the psyche of leadership to explore ways of generating significant voluntary creativity and emotional buy-in that is required to implement successful, fundamental and sustainable changes. It is not possible to do this without a thorough change of culture and this involves a cognitive change in both the individual and the collective will.

It is important to look at the factors that lie behind the growing power of individual stakeholder groups and the increasingly complex links between them. These include globalization and the battles being fought by organizations on a global stage for custom, for capital, for employees with the right skills and attitudes, and even for their license to operate in local communities. Mergers and acquisitions are leading to the blurring of distinctions between competitor, customer and supplier, making each player more influential on the other.

Employees are becoming more empowered and are taking more responsibility for improved performance – individually and collectively – and are demanding more of a say in what happens around them.

Customers are also becoming more sophisticated. On every aspect of the value chain, from price and product to convenience and service, today's customer is better informed, has more choice and is becoming more demanding.

The information revolution is making organizations more transparent and people are better able to react quickly to events such as a huge drop in share prices, profit alerts and mergers or take-overs.

Ethics and corporate integrity are playing key roles in stakeholder management: from environmental issues, to animal rights, to individual pensions. More and more organizations are beginning to look beyond their boundaries and are wishing to influence society at large. They are becoming more involved in community, social and educational initiatives. To this end, businesses are beginning to develop more holistic models with a stakeholder component such as the European Foundation for Quality Management's framework.

Commenting on its report 'What Price Reputation?' published in November 1997, the magazine *Management Today* expresses it well:

> "The days when companies could do as they pleased, fly in the face of public opinion, turn a blind ear to the cries of staff, routinely give 'no comment' to the press and speak to the City only via their profit margins are long gone ... in the 1990s corporate reputation has become more important and more vulnerable than ever before."

Mission impossible without commitment

A major concern for those leading change is how to generate the required level of commitment from the stakeholders. Knowledge, understanding and involvement precede commitment. Before people can be asked to commit time, budget and resources to achieving change, they must understand what it will take and what is expected of them. Vague commitments of support lead to major conflicts and deep-seated mistrust later. Leaders can come up with the best PowerPoint presentations on the change initiative that show sound strategic vision and commercial logic – but it will not work if they cannot get their employees and other strategic stakeholders to understand what they are doing and why; get their buy-in into the vision; and constantly generate excitement and passion about the vision.

Corporate commitment must also be seen as credible. Stakeholders may consider the change initiative to be of low importance if the leadership is sending out mixed signals. You can always tell when the corporate leadership is going through the motions, it is the bored look on the CEO's face whenever the topic is brought up. Where leadership is not *"walking the talk"* everyone will pay lip service to the change program, and old values, patterns of behavior and inertia will make the mission impossible.

Cultural change

It is amazing how some who have had the mantle of leadership thrust upon them still believe (or act as if they believe) that successful change can be implemented where the existing culture is an obsolete and disabling one. It is common to find that some leaders tend to shy away from this most emotional and crucial aspect of leading and implementing change. This is where the pain is, where the battle is fought, and it takes time and investment of other key resources.

This is the uncomfortable point that determines whether the change will fail or succeed. The reality that some leaders fail to grasp is that change is an emotional proposition on both the individual and organizational level. According to Jeanie Daniel Duck: "rarely do people change their behavior just because they know they should. It is easier to change when we know there will be a positive pay-off or negative consequence."[1]

Cultural change involves an organization unlearning unproductive and disabling patterns of behavior and learning better, effective ways of performing for the purpose of organizational effectiveness. Yet it is this necessary organizational learning that is most painful and the most resisted because as Carl Rogers puts it: "Learning which involves a change in self-organization – in the perception of self – is threatening and tends to be resisted."

Also, it is often the case that the change leader thinks the cultural change that needs to take place in order to effect fundamental, successful change, is a change that needs to be *done to others* and not to leadership, because after holding several CEO or senior management positions *leadership knows best*!

So, having a fabulous business plan is just the beginning, the child's play. For the leader to believe in the vision; to generate a collective belief in it; to be able to package it and to sell it; and to have the perseverance and the resilience to make it work – these are the areas where the change leaders roll up their sleeves and *get dirty*.

With the right investment, an organization that is led by dynamic people can effect profoundly successful change in a remarkably short time.

This is exactly what Gerhard Schulmeyer did when he came to Siemens Nixdorf in the late summer of 1994.

EXHIBIT 2

Embarking on cultural change is a brave, uncharted step for a change leader and this is because transforming a corporation through cultural, behavioral and organizational change takes guts, grit and time. In the early 1990s Siemens Nixdorf was a major loser on the business chessboard. Today, it is the largest European player in data processing and customer relationship management; and the continent's number two in software, services and mainframes. The program of development is still ongoing, with employees taking the responsibility for improving their business processes, effectively implementing their own re-engineering, and sharing the corporate knowledge and ideas on the corporate intranet.

Gerhard Schulmeyer, a veteran of business transformation, knew that if processes were re-engineered before a fundamental cultural change, the change program would be stunted and shafted. So he put the cultural change first on his agenda of business transformation. This meant mobilizing all the employees behind the vision, a process to which he allocated investment in terms of resources. He spent a great deal of his time meeting employees, identifying change leaders and other strategic stakeholders to get buy-in – and to honestly discuss the measures that were needed to dig the company out of the financial and organizational mess it was in, and the behavioral changes required to accomplish the vision.

In Schulmeyer's case, he put cultural change ahead of process change but he built in "fair practice." This is the process that ensures that employees and other stakeholders understand exactly the processes by which decisions are made, even if not everyone agrees with them.

Managing the speed of change

Here is a real challenge: how do you transform your business into a high-performance, high-profit, high-satisfaction enterprise in a remarkably short time?

Gone are the days when leaders used to wait for inspiration! These days it is essential for a leader to be able to skillfully read and interpret situations and to react appropriately and in time. Inspiration and speed go hand in hand. Leaders do not have the luxury of waiting to be inspired and motivated – inspiration catches up with the best leaders whilst in action.

One of the challenges facing organizations is the speed at which to develop, be it new products, new processes, new systems, or new technology. Should the planned change be evolutionary in nature or revolutionary? Do we start small or go for the *big bang* approach? Knowing what must be changed within the organization is not enough. More important is knowing how to make the changes quickly, effectively, economically and with as little as possible bloodshed in the boardroom and canteens.

The difficulty with the high speed of change needed to retain a competitive edge today can be related to the fact that whilst times and business are changing, people are still playing catch-up because they have not been conditioned to rapid pace. This mismatch between the rapid rate of change and the expectations of the people is usually one of the major causes of tension in change programs.

Organizations are faced with the most challenging task of coping with the rapid flux of change created by an unstable economy; yet some organizations remain trapped in the old ways doing things – thus sending the wrong signals to their employees. For the dinosaurs to survive, they will have to be transformed into minimal living organisms that possess the flexibility, agility and the capability to respond faster to change; and to continually evolve and re-create themselves. A good reference book on this topic is *Managing at the Speed of Change*, by Daryl Conner.[2]

Resilience

The increasing rate of major changes has forever transformed the business skyline. Everywhere you look there are major changes taking place and our globe shrinks day by day, consequently pushing businesses to the competitive limit.

''Resilience'' means being capable to bounce back, whether you are going through stressful situations or not. It is the ability not just to survive change, but to actually bounce back stronger than before its challenge.

Beyond the obvious necessity of making sound decisions, developing personal and organizational resilience is the single most important competency in increasing an organization's competitive edge during turbulent times. Resilience is the essential component that transforms the mystery of change into a manageable process. It is often what distinguishes change ''winners,'' those whose projects are implemented on time and within budgets – from ''losers'' – those who achieve short-term superficial change or none at all.

Leaders have to learn the art of building and leading resilient organizations that has the ability to consistently succeed in unpredictable and contested environments. Leaders can help their organizations in the following ways.

» Providing employees with a supportive environment that encourages readiness for change. Change is painful enough when it is not inflicted, as every change alters our lives and worldview in one way or the other. Even when change is positive there still needs to be a period of acceptance and adjustment. Leaders need to be sensitive to the impact of change on the people; and develop appropriate support mechanisms to lessen the pain. When people are involved in the change process and have external contact with their environments, they find it easier to be an active part of the change and to be able to deal with the speed of the change.

» Leaders must be careful not to overload employees with too much change all at once. Leaders must be aware of and pay particular attention to the speed and the nature of change. They must develop and put in place processes and mechanisms that can help shorten the phase of *pain*, and minimize the length of the phase. Change must not be for the sake of change alone. Leaders can ensure that their strategic change decisions are those that are truly imperative to the prosperity and good health of the organization.

» Leaders should build implementation plans for each phase of the change. Having tailored plans for each phase helps to lessen employee resistance and generates the right level of commitment to maximize the chances of the change becoming a success.

On an individual level, every change leader needs large doses of resilience (as a matter of fact, this is one thing you cannot overdose on). Businesses are now realizing that resilience is critical in times of change, and change being an emotional proposition can cause emotional overload and crashing where there is a low level or lack of resilience.

The resilience efforts come none too soon, said Rex Gatto. Gatto says a "perfect storm" is brewing as managers and workers deal with various pressures.

"You know how in the movie, all the elements came together at precisely the right time to create the 'perfect storm?' Well, that's what's taking place in business today," he said. "A lot of changes are taking place all the time, and it can be painful. Global competition, the technology explosion, customer demands, the frantic pace of business – all these variables are creating an emotional perfect storm.

And professionals everywhere are struggling to keep their heads above water."

Increasingly, the word "resilience" is creeping into business language and organizations such as 3M are building resilience training into their training programs.

Managing complexity

The theories of chaos and complexity from science are being increasingly applied to organizational and social life. Some of these ideas include:

» order leaps out of disorder;
» the butterfly effect;
» large unpredictable consequences flow from tiny, microscopic events in systems; and
» chaos leads to its twin science of complexity.

Other new perspectives include:

» emergence: that is the belief that the future emerges continuously and unpredictably out of the present;
» self-organization: the process of stimulating creativity and innovation; and
» cyclical, not linear: a challenge to ideas of cause and effect.

Change brings a lot of issues to the fore, not least the dilemma of understanding and managing complexity. The understanding is based on the ability to see patterns of interdependency underlying problems and to distinguish short- from long-term consequences of actions (based on Systems Thinking).

This reminds me of an analogy based on a poem in Eugene Guillevic's *Selected Poems*[3] (see Fig. 6.1).

In their recent book, *Harnessing Complexity*,[4] Robert Axelrod and Michael Cohen, proposed the Complex Adaptive Systems approach. This approach was drawn from business, information technology, epidemiology and other areas. A Complex Adaptive System is one in which many participants interact in intricate ways that continually reshape their collective future. In such systems, these participants keep re-visiting their vision, revising their strategies, trying to adapt to the

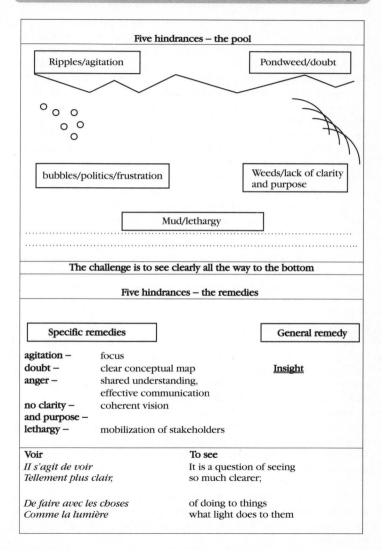

Fig. 6.1 Five hindrances: adapted from Eugene Guillevic's *Selected Poems*.

ever-changing circumstances that surround them. As they so do, they constantly change the circumstances to which other participants are trying to adapt.

Complexity exists in all domains of our world, in our private lives and in our public lives. When people ask how they can control complexity the unsaid question is: how can I eliminate complexity from my life?

However, it is not possible to remove complexity completely from our lives or from our organizations. This is because human beings are basically complex creatures and nothing can change this fundamental fact. Needless to say (but I shall say it anyway), because we are complex beings, it follows that organizations are complex adaptive systems. Not systems in the mechanical sense, but as in living organisms that are all the time connecting, interacting, expanding, contracting – constantly changing in response to changes in their circumstances and environment in ways that enable them to maintain their identity.

The concepts and questions this approach generates are as follows.

» Variation: what is the right balance between variety and uniformity?
» Interaction: what should interact with what, and when?
» Selection: what agents or strategies should be copied or weeded out?

Ironically, complexity itself does allow for techniques that promote effective adaptation, such as systems thinking. The nature of systems thinking makes it extremely effective on the most difficult types of problems to solve: those involving complex and complicated issues that have a great deal of dependence on historical issues, or on the actions of other people; and those arising from ineffective co-ordination and communication among those involved.

Most change in complex systems is emergent. This is to say it comes about as a result of interactions between the *agents* in the system. The *agents* are people – and people are in themselves complex organisms. The Complexity Theory suggests that when there is enough connectivity between the agents, emergence of fundamental and sustainable change is likely to occur spontaneously.

Change leaders should move away from trying to *change* organizations and instead look at how they might help them become ready for change – that is, they should move to a state of *self-organized criticality*.

Rather than focus all their energies on the impossible, that is, eliminating complexities, change leaders should explore how the dynamism of a Complex Adaptive System (this will involve spending some time in *the swamp*) can be used for productive ends by building new connections and relationships so that a process of self-organization can evolve.

By so doing, they should be able to alter the way they view the *complexity*, positively re-frame the complexity, and develop the ability to make effective decisions in a world of rapid change. This chapter cannot dig deeper into the issue of Complexity and Systems Thinking but Chapter 9 includes some useful resources on the subject.

The soul of leadership

The *San Francisco Chronicle* reported last year that there were about 322 citations for the word "soul" in the current edition of *Books in Print*. This is amazing but not unexpected.

As the nature of work continues to be influenced by factors such as globalization, mergers, empowered employees, the Net and others, there is an increasing growth in the area of how people wish to be led and the attributes they seek in those who lead them. It is not uncommon these days to see a rebellion in some organizations against the "android" mentality unleashed by some leaders. Lately there have been questions about the lack of emotions behind leadership, a significant shift, as the common question during any change program is: "What does this mean for me, as an individual and who cares?" As Eileen McDargh said in an article: "Workers are no longer willing to rent themselves to a job to survive to the weekend." Rather, this term "soul" implies looking for a deeper purpose behind work other than just gaining a paycheck. It also implies that people want to be identified as whole individuals, with brains, hearts, *and* souls waiting to be opened within the workplace (with the exception of the zombies).

Daniel Goleman, in his book *Emotional Intelligence*,[5] sparked off the debate on this often neglected but crucial factor in leadership. I have worked alongside consultants and leaders who have practiced what I call *"soul-less leadership."* To win the hearts of those one wishes to lead, you have to understand where they are coming from and where they wish to go to – individually and with the organization. As a leader, one can breed robots who clock in and out, having ticked the boxes for the day. However, this does not create an atrium for creativity, dynamism, continuous organizational learning or sustainable growth. As work patterns change and employees seek a greater degree of control over their destinies, they are beginning to question their purpose and how that purpose is aligned with that of the organization. If there is a huge discrepancy between where the *heart* of the organization wants to go and where the *head* wants to go, bodies will walk.

I agree with Former Secretary of State (USA) Robert McNamara, who said: "Brains are like hearts; they usually go where they are appreciated."

In the change leadership context, whilst I would not go as far as Daniel Goleman to suggest that emotional intelligence predicts about 80 percent of a person's success in life or as a change leader, I can say that it is a critical leadership quality. Emotional intelligence has its roots in the concept of "social intelligence," first identified by E.L. Thorndike in 1920. Thorndike defined social intelligence as the "ability to understand and manage men and women, boys and girls – to act wisely in human relations." So basic, so fundamental.

In 1983, Howard Gardner, a Harvard University professor of education and author, added to this debate by including inter- and intrapersonal intelligences in his theory of multiple intelligences. These two intelligences make up social intelligence. He defines them as follows:

> "**Inter**personal intelligence is the ability to understand other people: what motivates them, how they work, how to work cooperatively with them. Successful salespeople, politicians, teachers, clinicians, and religious leaders are all likely to be individuals with high degrees of interpersonal intelligence. **Intra**personal intelligence ... is a correlative ability, turned inward. It is a capacity to form an accurate, veridical model of oneself and to be able to use that model to operate effectively in life."

According to Mayer & Salovey, emotional intelligence is "a type of social intelligence that involves the ability to monitor one's own and others' emotions, to discriminate among them, and to use the information to guide one's thinking and actions."[6] Furthermore, it is about being able to relate to others, to understand where they are coming from, and to be able to *walk in their shoes*.

Social scientists are beginning to uncover the strong relationship between emotional intelligence and other phenomena, such as change leadership, organizational performance and effectiveness, individual performance, and change management, to name a few. No doubt, this is a concept that has come to stay. Chapter 10 further explores this side of leading change, as well as other related concepts for change leadership success.

NOTES

1 Quoted by Stephen Overell in his article "The agony of transformation" *Financial Times*, May 2, 2001, p. 15.
2 Conner, D. (1993) *Managing at the Speed of Change*. John Wiley & Sons, New York.
3 Guillevic, E. (1969) *Selected Poems*, tr. *Denise Levertov*. New Directions, New York.
4 Axelrod, R. &. Cohen, M.D. (2000) *Harnessing Complexity: Organizational Implications of a Scientific Frontier*. Simon & Schuster, New York.
5 Goleman, D. (1995) *Emotional Intelligence*. Bantam Books, New York.
6 Salovey, P. & Mayer, J.D. (1993) "The Intelligence of Emotional Intelligence." *Intelligence*, **17**, pp. 433–442.

Leading Change In Practice

Real-life case studies on what change leaders are doing in the United States of America, Europe and Asia; including lessons learnt.

"It doesn't matter what I believe, it only matters what I can prove."
A Few Good Men directed by Rob Reiner, 1992.

This chapter provides some examples of best change leadership principles in practice. They have been selected to provide a diverse range of effective change leadership approaches in the real world – in real time.

The following three case studies demonstrate what is being done by leading organizations, and the results of their innovative, and often painful experiences in the wilderness.

THE CISCO CASE STUDY

Empowering employees

The workforce optimization program at Cisco empowers staff and saves the company millions each year.

» GOALS. Create a workforce optimization program that empowers employees, streamlines administrative tasks, provides management with vital information, and promotes a positive corporate culture.
» STRATEGY. Use the Web to create a globally distributed, self-service employee portal with user-friendly applications.
» RESULTS. An annual saving of more than $86 million and one of the industry's lowest turnover rates.

The new hire dashboard

It's a small drama played out thousands of times each day in corporate offices around the world. The new hire plunks down her boxes in an empty cubicle or office, thrilled at the start of a new job, but sweaty-palmed and anxious about the prospect of adapting to a new corporate culture. Traditionally, the only resources available were a sympathetic co-worker and a thick employee manual. But new hires at Cisco have another tool that can help.

It's called the "new hire dashboard" – an easy-to-use intranet portal that provides tips on everything from setting up an e-mail account to establishing a 401(k) plan. Figuring that the dashboard saves new hires at least 15 minutes per day for a three-month ramping-up period, the annual saving for this project alone is in excess of $11mn per year for Cisco.

The dashboard is just one element of the Cisco workforce optimization campaign, forming an "Internet culture" that empowers employees and saves the company at least $86mn annually.

The applications optimize tasks from the routine to the complex, and even improve communications and learning – all enabled by an integrated, secure global network.

"Any time we can get information to people that is personal, that's empowering. Any time we can remove an intermediary, that's empowering. And any time we can give employees the decision-support tools to analyze and improve their situation, that's empowering. So our goal was to create an environment where employees have the right information at the right time, and the ability to act on it," says Marianne Jackson, Cisco vice president of human resources.

Cisco Employee Connection

Most Cisco employees begin their workday with the browser-based workforce optimization command center, known as the Cisco Employee Connection. It's here that employees compare meeting schedules, procure office equipment, request workplace repairs or technical assistance, review employee benefits, make business travel arrangements, attend distance-learning classes, and even order catered items for upcoming meetings.

And while the financial savings have been impressive, workforce optimization has other significant advantages, including employee empowerment, streamlined administration, and improved recruiting and benefits management.

Employee empowerment

Self-service via the Web lets employees do their jobs instead of spending valuable time processing paperwork or searching for information. And that's good for business, says Sharon Meaney, IS/business liaison for the Cisco Workplace Resources intranet site.

"On our site employees can do everything from requesting a cubicle reassignment to getting new office keys," Meaney says. "They can place a service request for building maintenance, order catering for a meeting, and track incoming package shipments." The site receives about 250,000 hits each month, with 36% of all hits clicking through to the site's extensive section of maps and building floor plans.

Meaney is now working with an extended workplace resources e-business team to improve the site with features that allow users to personalize a Workplace Resources portal.

Employees are also empowered when they learn. Cisco e-learning initiatives enable employees to learn when, where, and how they want to. Programs run the gamut from help-desk style knowledge-based systems to just-in-time e-learning and virtual classrooms.

Specialized learning portals

Cisco has created formal learning portals for key areas of its business, including manufacturing, worldwide customer service, field sales, company audit, and channel sales. And Cisco has used e-learning to address certification needs and executive education.

Managers can track an employee's learning experience from the initial student profile or resume through the learning history to the impact the learning has on the business.

Streamlined administration

Perhaps the most visibly beneficial employee self-service application at Cisco is Metro, the travel/expense reporting application that allows employees to report expenses on an electronic expense account form. Reimbursement goes directly into the employee's checking account within two days, in contrast to the three weeks the old paper process took.

Capital savings

Many organizations spend up to 60 percent of their revenues on indirect goods and services, such as office and electronic supplies. Yet this large expense category has been virtually ignored by managerial cost cutters and bypassed by enterprise resource planning systems, according to a recent study by market research firm Killen and Associates.

Before Cisco implemented a Web-based procurement solution, it, too, was wasting millions of dollars purchasing non-essential items. The problem was compounded by the company's tremendous growth. The challenge required Cisco to revolutionize the way it bought goods and services.

Since Cisco integrated its procurement solution with those of People-Soft, Oracle, and Ariba, the company has slashed purchasing transaction costs in half. This has eliminated nearly 50,000 manual transactions and saved approximately $3mn in administrative costs. And even though the number of transactions has doubled every year since 1997, the company's staffing needs have been greatly reduced; the purchasing department went from three clerks to two, and routing clerks, whose only job was to hand-carry purchase requests from approver to approver, are rarely necessary. Cisco estimates savings to be nearly $110mn since it implemented better purchasing practices in 1997.

Improved recruiting and benefits management

The top recruiting goal at Cisco is simple, yet ambitious: to develop an environment that will attract and retain the top 10 percent of available professionals in the industry. Today more than 70 percent of all resumes received by Cisco are submitted through the Web. Combined with other recruiting solutions, this has contributed to a $2mn financial benefit for Cisco.

Inspired leadership

Workforce optimization programs are a two-way informational street. The Cisco manager dashboard, Cafi Mocha, and other decision-support systems provide executives with the latest information from across the enterprise in such critical areas as time/labor tracking, recruitment, and budget analysis.

"Every action that can be taken by managers can be done online automatically. So rather than second-guess every management decision, we can give managers a little bandwidth for decision making and audit them if there's a problem," Cisco manager, Dcamp says.

The company's Leadership Express is a portal of self-directed learning for Cisco managers, providing management tools and articles on leadership, searchable by topic.

Cisco has seen impressive results from its workforce optimization programs, but the company isn't resting on its laurels. Instead, it's developing new programs and enhancing current programs to extend the model even further.

Case Study by Eric J. Adams, Petaluma, California[1]

THE ROYAL/DUTCH SHELL CASE STUDY

Grassroots leadership

Steve Miller of Royal Dutch/Shell offers a powerful model of what leadership means – a recognition that commitment and creativity come from all parts and all levels of an organization.

Grassroots leadership is not a term you would ordinarily apply to Royal Dutch/Shell. With a current market capitalization of $178bn, $128bn in annual revenues, 101,000 employees, and operations in 130 countries around the globe, Royal Dutch/Shell is often cited as one of the world's largest businesses – but never as one of the fastest. With its 90-year history, its deep sense of tradition, and its carefully structured ways of doing things, Royal Dutch/Shell is often praised as a model of consistency and longevity – but never as one of creativity or innovation.

Steve Miller, 52, group managing director of the Royal Dutch/Shell group of companies meant to change all that when he joined Shell's Committee of Managing Directors, the senior leaders who guide the day-to-day activities of the Shell Group, in 1996, two years after the company had launched a program designed to transform the organization. But after two years of reorganizing, downsizing, and attending workshops, Shell managers had little to show for their efforts. The company's financial performance inched up – but employee morale at corporate headquarters in London and The Hague continued to slip. And for people in the field – "at the coal face," to use the term that Shell applies to its frontline activities – everything looked like business as usual.

Miller had observed Shell's efforts to transform itself one layer of management at a time, and he concluded that he would have to reach around the resistant bureaucracy and involve those at the front lines of the company. But the sheer size of the operation made this a daunting prospect. Shell's 47,000 filling stations, for example, serve about 10 million customers each day. And the downstream business consisting of dozens of product lines, from fuels to lubricants to asphalt, and of operations stretching from supply and trading to manufacturing and marketing, faced the gravest of competitive threats: hypermarkets in Europe, new competitors worldwide, and demanding global customers. Starting in 1997, Miller devoted more than 50 percent of his time to work directly with grassroots employees to respond to this new competitive situation.

His approach adds a new chapter to the art and science of grassroots leadership. Aided by a business model developed by Larry Selden of the Columbia Business School, and supported by process-design assistance from Noel Tichy of the University of Michigan Business School, Miller and his colleagues at Shell evolved a system that is as revolutionary in the world of sales and marketing as Toyota's innovations in total quality management were in the manufacturing world two decades ago.

Most important, Miller's approach offers a model of grassroots leadership that any leader in any company can adopt.

Why he needed to rethink the basics of leadership

Miller believed that Shell needed a new definition of leadership and a new approach to providing it. In his words:

> "in the past, the leader was the guy with the answers. Today, if you're going to have a successful company, you have to recognize that no leader can possibly have all the answers. The leader may have a vision. But the actual solutions about how best to meet the challenges of the moment have to be made by the people closest to the action – the people at the coal face.
>
> "The leader has to find the way to empower these frontline people, to challenge them, to provide them with the resources they need, and then to hold them accountable. As they struggle with the details of this challenge, the leader becomes their coach, teacher, and facilitator. Change how you define leadership, and you change how you run a company. Once the folks at the grass roots find that they own the problem, they find that they also own the answer – and they improve things very quickly, very aggressively, and very creatively, with a lot more ideas than the old-style leader could ever hand down from headquarters."

Why he adopted a grassroots approach

"Shell's transformation program got started because headquarters and the operating companies couldn't agree on how we were going to adapt to a rapidly changing world. How would we respond to the Information Age? We needed something to give us an energy transfusion and to remind us that we could play at a more competitive level. Shell has always been a wholesaler. But every service station represents a commercial opportunity that any retailer would envy. Our task was to tap the potential of that real estate, and we needed our frontline troops to pull it off."

The grassroots program

Miller and his co-leaders brought six- to eight-person teams from a half-dozen operating companies worldwide into an intense "retailing boot camp." Here's one example, from Malaysia.

In an effort to improve service-station revenues along major highways, cross-functional teams that included a dealer, a union trucker, and four or five marketing executives were brought in. The first five-day workshop introduced the model and the leadership skills the team would need to enlist co-workers back home, and prepared the participants to apply the new tools to a local market opportunity. That could mean improved performance at filling stations on the major roadways in Malaysia, or selling liquefied natural gas elsewhere in Asia.

Then those teams went home – while another group of teams rotated in. For the next 60 days, the first set of teams worked on developing business plans. Then they came back to boot camp for a peer-review challenge. At the end of the third workshop, each team sat with Millar and his team in a "fishbowl" to review its business plan, while the other teams watched. The peer pressure and the learning were intense. At the end of that session, the teams went back for another 60 days to put their ideas into action. Then they came back for a follow-up to analyze both breakdowns and breakthroughs.

Results

There is evidence of positive results all around the world. For instance, Shell's business in France was in terrible shape. They were in the red and losing market share. The advent of hypermarkets had changed the game, and Shell wasn't responding effectively to this new competitive threat. Fifty percent of the fuel market disappeared in two years! They either had to find a way to become profitable and to grow, or they had to exit – because the way they were going, they couldn't stay in the game much longer.

Now, if you asked the leader back in headquarters, "What's the answer?" the honest response would be "I don't know." What Shell did instead was bring together a cross-functional team from France, provide the people on it with resources to analyze the problem, offer them a business model to help them understand retail competition better – and then challenge them to come up with ways not just to survive but also to grow.

When the business closed its books for 1997, it recorded double-digit profitability, exceeded its growth target, and expected double-digit growth for 1998. But for Miller there was something even more important: "The manager told me that when he and his co-workers started to work on the problem, they were terrified. They didn't know how they could solve it. Now they believe in themselves. As a result of this effort, they've got a whole new company."

The challenge of grassroots leadership

» First, putting oneself on the line with one's peers and not playing the classic "managing director" role.

» Entrusting people with the vision and believing in them to *make it happen.*

» Finally, the scariest part is letting go, in particular, letting go of the old style of control.

On being a leader/teacher

According to Miller, a teacher first needs to know his or her material forward, backward, inside, and out.

Second, as a leader and as a teacher, you've got to open yourself up. You simply have to make it personal. But real teaching means giving of yourself and creating a personal connection.

Follow-ups

Miller does a lot of field visits – for example, going on bus rides with teams, and talking to customers.

He and his team write down their impressions and go over what they have learnt from the visits. They have found this to be a great learning tool – it breaks down the barriers between functions. They learn collectively, they learn to understand the customer, and they share the responsibility to fix the customer's problems – whether they're in sales or accounting.

Take-away on leadership and change

As people move up in organizations, they get further away from the work that goes on in the field, and as a result, they tend to devalue it. People get caught up in broad strategic issues, legal issues, stakeholder issues. But what really drives a business is the work that goes on down at the coal face. It's reliability, it's producing to specification, it's delivering to the customer.

Now, if that's true, then being connected to people in the field is even more critical. They need all the support leaders can give them. They need a common understanding of where they're going, and they need a common understanding of the business. That's what drives execution. And it's what provides the discipline in a grassroots change program.

Based on an interview by Richard Pascale[2]

THE KOMATSU CASE STUDY – RYOICHI KAWAI'S LEADERSHIP

Leading business transformation

This case study outlines the role played by Ryoichi Kawai in building a company that was able to challenge industry leader Caterpillar.

In late January 1985 chairman Ryoichi Kawai of Komatsu Limited, the world's second largest earth-moving equipment company, saw the quarterly financial results of Caterpillar Tractor Co. (Cat), its arch-rival. With his understanding of the industry and of his competitor's problems, he was not surprised to see Cat's losses continuing, but he had not expected the figure to be so high. The $251mn fourth-quarter loss brought the company's full year loss to $428mn, closing out Cat's third straight unprofitable year. Although Komatsu appeared to be closing in on a competitor that had long dominated the industry, Kawai knew Cat would fight hard to regain its pre-eminent position. The industry structure was changing, and Kawai realized it might be time to re-appraise Komatsu's competitive strategy. "After all" mused Kawai, "one important lesson to be drawn from Cat's decline is that *success today does not necessarily imply success tomorrow*."

Demand for earth-moving equipment sprang primarily from construction and mining. Worldwide sales totaled approximately $14 to $15bn during the early 1980s. Mining accounted for almost 30 percent of demand. Patterns of mineral production had been altered by nationalization of mines in developing countries during the 1960s and 1970s, which led to the opening of new mines in politically safer countries such as Canada and Australia. The market leader, by a large margin, was Caterpillar, based in Peoria, Illinois. In the 1980s Caterpillar began to struggle and it particularly faced a major challenge in its labor relations.

It was in this broad context that Komatsu found itself in the mid-1990s. In 1984, the Osaka-based company with its headquarters in Tokyo had consolidated net sales in excess of $3bn. Over 80 percent of the sales emanated from the earth-moving equipment sector, yet only two decades earlier, Komatsu had been just one of many small local equipment manufacturers living in the shadow of Cat.

Komatsu was established in 1921 as a specialized producer of mining equipment. The company's basic philosophy since its earliest days emphasized the need to export. Yashinari Kawai, Komatsu's president in the 1960s, was determined to take advantage of the Japanese government's requirement that foreign companies help Japanese companies in return for access to Japan's markets. He planned to make his company a world-class competitor. As part of his mission, he launched one of the first quality upgrading programs to reflect the Total Quality Control concept. All personnel, from top management to every worker on the assembly line were expected to strive for total quality control.

In 1964, Ryoichi Kawai succeeded his father as chairman, and set about furthering the goals the older man had set.

First, he launched Project A: to upgrade the quality of small and medium-sized bulldozers, Komatsu's primary domestic market product. He told staff to ignore the costs and produce world-standard products; and to disregard the Japanese Industrial Standards (JIS).

» The first batch of upgraded products reached the market in 1966, with spectacular results.

» As a result of the cost reductions, between 1965 and 1970 the company increased its domestic market share from 50 to 65 percent even as the Mitsubishi–Caterpillar joint venture began production in Japan.

» In addition, the change initiative greatly improved the quality of work within the company. A crisis atmosphere prevailed in the company when the project was being implemented, resulting in a spirit of unity between the management and staff. This was perhaps the most valuable achievement of the project.

In 1972 Kawai launched Project B: to boost exports by improving the large bulldozer, the company's main export item. As in Project A, the aim was to upgrade quality and reliability, bringing large bulldozer models up to world standards, then to work on cost reductions. During the early 1970s the company's research and development efforts continued apace with attention to basic research as well as product development.

By 1976, the Japanese market was highly concentrated, with Komatsu taking a 60 percent share and the Mitsubishi–Cat joint venture left with slightly over 30 percent. Kawai then decided to focus on improving the competitiveness of Komatsu's products.

First, he initiated a four-part cost reduction plan, beginning with the "V-10 campaign." The V-10 goal was to reduce costs by 10 percent while maintaining or improving product quality. The second part of the plan called for reducing the number of parts by over 20 percent. The third part aimed at value engineering, specifically focusing on redesigning the products to gain economies in materials or manufacturing. The fourth part was a radicalization of the manufacturing system. By the end of the decade, the company was well on its way to achieving all these goals.

To celebrate Komatsu's 60th anniversary in 1981, Kawai launched a new project called EPOCHS (Efficient Production-Oriented Choice Specifications). The new project's aim was to "improve production efficiency without reducing the number of product specifications required by the market." By the end of 1983, the company's manufacturing had become fully integrated, producing all of its components and parts in-house (it was the largest producer of steel castings in Japan, for example). Throughout the expansion, Kawai continued to emphasize a strong commitment to research and development.

By 1985, Komatsu managers had good reasons to be proud of their company's records over the previous two decades. It still held a 60 percent share in Japan; the company's domestic sales and service network was acknowledged to be the most extensive and efficient in Japan; and exports had expanded to represent well over half of Komatsu's total sales.

By the 1980s, Komatsu's management process had developed several unique characteristics. Over the years, Ryoichi Kawai had developed what he termed the "PDCA" (Plan, Do, Check, and Act) management cycle. The starting point for the PDCA cycle was the long-term plan announced by the top management team, and the company president's policy statement issued at the beginning of the year. Kawai referred to this as "management by policy," which he then explained:

> "Personally, I believe that a company must always be innovative. To this end, the basic policy and value of the target must be clarified so that all the staff members can fully understand what the company is aiming for in a specific time period. This is the purpose of the management by policy system."

Thus, a plan is made, it is executed, its results are checked, and then new actions are planned. Every activity is based on this cycle, including company-wide management control systems. Corporate ability to achieve the targets set improves. These steps also improve the workers' morale and management's leadership.

Ryoichi Kawai viewed the development of the management process and organizational culture as a leader's most important responsibility:

> "A human being donates his energy to work in order to enjoy and lead an enriched life ... We think that it is necessary to satisfy the worker's monetary and other needs simultaneously. First of all, there is the satisfaction in the achievement in work. Second, there is the satisfaction of collaborating with a colleague and receiving the approval of others. Third, there is the satisfaction of witnessing an organization grow and achieve maturity. It is satisfaction, pride, and consciousness toward participation that

make workers feel that they are contributing to a great objective and are doing important work in the company.''

Komatsu had a long history of good labor relations, which the company believed was important to its ability to improve productivity and achieve cost competitiveness. Statistics compiled by Nomura Securities confirm this.

Within Komatsu, Kawai was viewed almost as a deity, whose primary role was *leadership*. He not only provided a coherent vision and goals, but he focused the organization on product quality and cost, especially through effective team-work. His attitude was: "We've got to continually do better." He delegated day-to-day operations, giving a great deal of freedom and allowing ideas and projects to bubble up. But once they did, he and the board *actively* participated in deciding what the company would do.

As a leader, Kawai:

» had frequent personal contact with line and staff managers at different levels;
» personally participated in a company-wide program of quality control and audit;
» attended monthly quality control guidance meetings led by Tokyo University professor Kaoru Ishikawa; and
» believed that the involvement of top management made a great difference and so he personally led the top management group.

In Kawai's own words,

> "Eternal vigilance is not the price of liberty alone. It is also the price of prosperity."
>
> *A summary of a case study by Professor A. Bartlett*[3]

The above case studies go to show that "where there is a will, there is a way." It illustrates leaders who are willing to address the following.

» **Unblock**. Where are we getting stuck? Why are we lagging behind? What is the minimum needed to open up our organization's life processes?
» **Enable**. How and where can we do things better and right?

» **Enhance**. How can we embed those things that we have learnt to do better in our everyday practice; and develop the agility and flexibility that leads to eternal vigilance, rigor and success?

For me, I have also learnt that:

» as a leader, if I make things TANGIBLE, I am likely to do it rather than try to take on the world;
» meanings come from specific work/things that move, regardless of the pace;
» we rationally calculate our continuous improvement, provided errors from the past are pounced upon and corrected; and
» as a leader, I need courage to challenge incomplete dominant paradigms; and fly in the face of tradition when there is a calling to so do.

NOTES

1 Case study covers business trends, strategies, and solutions. January 30, 2001.
2 Interview featured in *Fast Company* issue 14, p110. Richard Pascale was a faculty member at the Stanford Business School for 20 years and is now an associate fellow of Oxford University. Based in San Francisco, he is a well-known expert on corporate transformation.
3 Presented in "Caterpillar Tractor Co." No. 385–276, and Komatsu Ltd, No. 385–277, based on his work with Srinavasa Rangan. With permission from Harvard Business School (ECCH, Cranfield University, UK).

Key Concepts and Thinkers

A glossary of key concepts and thinkers on leading, implementing and institutionalizing change.

"Progressiveness is looking forward intelligently, looking within critically, and moving on incessantly."

Waldo Pondray Warren

There is a proliferation of literature on leadership, management, and change management. This chapter builds on previous chapters by providing an A to Z glossary of key concepts that pertain to effective and successful leadership of change, whatever the size of the change; and it introduces the key thought leaders in the field of change leadership. The final chapter of this book will provide some guidelines on leading change in *"real world"* sense.

PART A: A GLOSSARY OF KEY TERMS AND CONCEPTS IN LEADING CHANGE

Action learning

Action learning strongly positions the view that learning is the strategic variable in individual and organizational development and effectiveness; and it can be used as a tool for the quick acceleration of teamwork and for building communities of leaders for rapidly changing organizational conditions. The desired outcome of action learning is to enhance the organization's capacity to learn and change.

So the ultimate outcome desired from action learning is the generalization of the learning methods to the overall organizational culture, so that the organization's capacity to learn and therefore improve its responses to its changing environment is enhanced.

Belief

Change leaders have got to believe in the vision to the extent that they live it. Barry White, the famous songwriter and artist sang "practice what you preach." Kevin Roberts, chief executive of Saatchi and Saatchi Advertising Worldwide, using sports teams as an analogy, said: "teams also require inspirational players who can provide not only leadership and coaching, but inspire the organization with a belief in its own greatness."

Buy-in

Even if you have the greatest vision, greatest strategy, mightiest technology in the world, if your workforce does not buy into the vision it will all be in vain – and it will end in tears.

Collaborative enterprise

Collaborative has been described as a means for organizations to gain a competitive edge through maximization of the value of relationships, both inside and outside the organization. It is all embracing and it touches on all aspects of the enterprise, from strategy to front-operations. As David Harvey describes in a Business Intelligence White Paper:

> "the collaborative enterprise maximizes the potential of its relationships with competitors, customers, trading partners and employees to improve performance for mutual benefit."

Collaboration is a core concept of the knowledge management movement with its emphasis on communities of practice and other knowledge sharing activities. In a very real sense, the exchange of best-practice thinking, problem solving and ideas depends on a collaborative approach to business and management.

Change drivers

These are the driving forces behind an organization's desire or need to change. Examples are:

» "We must all be passionate about our support for customer service;"
» "Income growth is more likely to come through increased sales rather than cost reduction;" and
» "It is our aim to take £xmn of today's operating cost base."

Change levers

These are the elements that will influence the change: the enablers. They include financial incentives such as rewards, training and education, effective communications, knowledge management and so on. For example:

» transform the way we work to meet the demands of the increasingly competitive retail banking sector; and
» get better at managing, developing and expanding our customer base and product range.

To do this effectively we have to:

» develop our customer management information;
» create an integrated source of customer data and functionality;
» manage the interaction with customers consistently across multiple channels; and
» analyze our information and produce targeted products and services quickly.

Commitment

Leading change successfully and effectively requires commitment from everyone in an organization but it also demands clear targeting to achieve the desired aims and objectives of improving business performance. People must understand what is going to happen, why, to whom, when, what it will take and what is expected of them. The starting point in gaining commitment is to draw up a list of all the tasks that need to be carried out and then to assess the roles and responsibilities with those people involved. Then there should be an assessment of the quality of the resources (people, materials, technology, equipment, facilities, budget) that will be required on a task by task basis. Finally, the total commitment should be weighed against the anticipated benefits. Leaders should ask, "is it worth it?" The answer should determine their choice of action.

Communications

This subject is very popular yet, over and over again, change initiatives fail and business expectations fall short of expectations because of a communication vacuum. Nick Franchini said in an article in *Professional Manager*:[1]

"When organizational change takes place in a communication vacuum, all the stakeholders involved will draw their own conclusions about what it means to them. If there is 'no story' then individuals will figure out their own 'explanation' to fill the information gap."

Dr Richard Varey went on to say that "Communication is like a game of football." Just like football, there are rules and, in order to understand them, leaders need to understand the cultural values of those with whom they are communicating.

Contingency theories

Contingency theories basically all argue that the "right" or an effective leadership style varies according to the context. An example is Blake and Mouton's managerial grid, which has been very influential in organization development practice. Fielder, one of the leaders of the contingency school, offered a continuum ranging from task-focused to people-focused leadership. He argued that the most effective style depended on the quality of relationships, relative power position between the leader and the led and the nature of the task. He also argued that the style adopted is relatively stable and a feature of a leader's personality and could therefore be predicted. He distinguishes between task-oriented and relations-oriented leaders (LPC scale).

Cultural change

This is the most profound part of the change process and the most painful. It calls for complete behavioral change that embraces everyone in the organization; and aims to establish a set of values that places human behavior at the heart of the culture. Achieving cultural change takes time and this is because any major transition process will challenge the beliefs, attitudes and values of each individual in the organization. Even after the adoption of the "change", time is needed for adjustment. It is people who create and change organizations and *we may not know what the future holds, but we do know that human beings will be central players*. Culture is not imposed externally but internally, and any change program that attempts to change culture in a planned way is likely to miss the mark.

Empowerment

I view "empowerment" not as placing power in people but as enabling people to discover the power that lies within themselves; and creating an atrium for that power to be released and to be used creatively and innovatively. This also involves devolving not just tasks but decision-making and full responsibility.

Empowerment is an attribute of people and relations between people, and while it cannot be created by leadership, an organizational climate which encourages empowerment can be developed by leaders. It is worthy to note that as management and organizational theory has evolved in recent years, increasing consideration has been given to the concept that workplaces are essentially organizations of people brought together to pursue specific aims and purposes. Present experience does indicate that if the needs and the motivation of the workforce are satisfactorily related to the agreed aims and purposes of the organization, then effectiveness and efficiency will be the likely outcomes. The evidence from detailed research of well-run companies indicates that long-term profitability is best achieved where leadership and management processes are built around the pillars of personal empowerment and the active involvement of all the employees.

Engagement and stakeholder management

The influence of *all* stakeholder groups on the values, beliefs, policies, decisions and management of organizations is on the rise and here to stay. Today, the question for the leader of change/transformation is not whether they should be communicating with *this* or *that* stakeholder group but *how* to manage communication and to build commitment across stakeholder groups.

Informal leadership

This looks at behaviors associated with those who are not appointed to authority but assume leadership in other ways.

Inspirational theories

These include charismatic leaders and transformational leadership. The leader appeals to values and vision and enthuses others, raising confidence in others and motivating them for change.

Instrumental theories

These stress task- and person-oriented behavior (participation, delegation) by the leader to gain effective performance from others.

Learning

There has been a tendency in leaders to perceive learning as something that others do to us rather than as something we do for ourselves. Many definitions of learning point to a process of acquisition of knowledge during the processes of schooling and socialization. Thus success tends to be measured in terms of how quickly and how completely this process is completed. I say that learning is not merely a case of the deposition of knowledge but the interpretation and the application of the knowledge gained in a *real life context*. Furthermore, it is about kindling the knowledge that lies within us, that we do not know we know.

More than ever, today's leaders will have to be life-long learners who possess the determination and the courage to push and permeate boundaries; and to test new behaviors.

Learning organization

A learning organization is one in which people at all levels, individually and collectively, are continually increasing their capacity to produce results they really care about.

Why should organizations care? Because, the level of performance and improvement needed today requires learning, lots of learning. In most industries, in healthcare, and in most areas of government, there is no clear path to success, no clear path to follow.

What's in it for the people? *Learning to do* is enormously rewarding and personally satisfying. For those of us working in the field, the possibility of a win-win is part of the attraction. That is, the possibility of achieving extraordinary performance together with satisfaction and fulfillment for the individuals involved.

Are there any examples of learning organizations? Yes, but the learning organization is an ideal, a vision. Various organizations or parts of organizations achieve this in varying degree.

Several large corporations are attracted to this concept and are investing to support organizational learning.

Ownership

Ownership is ownership – there is no such thing as a "sense of owner-ship." Either you own something or you do not. Leaders need to be wary of assumptions about joint or corporate ownership of the change initiative.

Participative style of leadership

Hawthorne Studies and Kurt Lewin and Likert all propose that partici-pative styles of leadership lead to increased job satisfaction and higher performance.

Power

The subject of power remains a dominant one when leading change initiatives for *power* tends to create the paradigm for change. The questions are as follows.

» Who holds the paradigm anyway?
» Is the golden rule: he or she who holds the gold rule?
» In the principle of the Triple Loop of Learning, is might buttressed by right, or is right buttressed by might?

The acquisition and the use of power in itself are not bad; the question is about the best way to use the power. I have learnt that in order to influence, I have to have sufficient mandate, some degree of power. More importantly, I have to be comfortable about the degree and the usage of the power – for, as we know, *absolute power corrupts absolutely*.

Resilience

This is covered much more in Chapter 10. In essence, it is the ability to run the course; to persevere; and to give the change process all that is required of you; and to generate in your workforce all that is required of them. It requires discipline, and if we fail as leaders it is because we have not practiced the art of tenacity. It is linked to the principles of courage and of risk taking.

Sphere of influence

Stephen Covey, in his book, *The Seven Habits of Highly Effective People*,[2] points out that there are some matters over which you have control, and others that concern you, but where you can do nothing. They all belong to what he calls the Circle of Concern. Those you can affect are directly in the core, the Circle of Influence (see Fig. 8.1).

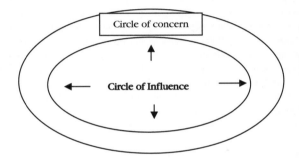

Fig. 8.1 The circle of influence and the circle of concern.

Within our Circle of Concern is the smaller Circle of Influence, which we should work to enlarge as much as possible.

Transformational leadership

Sometimes transformational leadership is used instead of charismatic leadership. This is a new paradigm and can offer a distinction between transformational (take people beyond self interest, raise motivation and moral commitment) and transactional (exchange of rewards/threats for compliance). Bennis and others also distinguish between transformational (doing the right thing) and transactional leadership (doing things right). This distinction is often quoted as the difference between management and leadership. This is a theme also picked up by Alan Hooper and John Potter, in their book, *Intelligent Leadership*.[2]

Values

In this new world where employees, customers and shareholders have a greater degree of choice, the issue of *values* is becoming a key factor in determining loyalty. In many organizations, one may have to work there for some time before one finds out what their real values are. And the key point is *real values* – that is, *core values*. Many leaders in organizations like to think, especially at board level, that they have clear values. Yet, upon closer exploration or even by accident, one finds that in some cases, most of these values only receive lip-service support – it is mostly rhetoric and not reality. I have personally experienced this and it can be devastating to employees, clients, and shareholders when the experience does not match the expectations. Integrity, trust and loyalty simply fly out of the window. This is not to suggest that values are set rigidly in stone, but that, as the work denotes, they are progressive and underpinned by integrity.

Vision

In his introduction to *Leaders on Leadership*, Stuart Crainer devotes a whole chapter to "the vision thing." To work, visions must motivate and sustain people through their implementation. Visions set the tone for change and carry forward the change, and those and that which needs to be changed. "One of the first duties is to create what I call atmosphere," observed the military leader, Montgomery. Vision is not an ethereal concept. Leaders must learn and master the art of bridging the gap between the noble aspirations of the vision and the day-to-day reality.

WIHTWWW

This is a key thinking for leaders of change and it means keeping a helicopter view of **W**hat **I**s **H**appening **T**o **W**hom **W**hy and **W**hen.

PART B: KEY THINKERS

This section contains information on a number of leadership theories and models.

Leadership continues to be a hot topic of debate even though interest in and discussions on what makes effective leaders is one as long as history itself. It is a topic of constant study and discussion where everyone seems to have a view and where definitions of leadership are as varied as the explanations. As businesses all over the world have to cope with endless waves of change, discussions on this subject are focusing more and more on leadership and change, vision building and empowering others. It is important to note that with few exceptions most of these theories originate from North America and do not usually take into account important issues such as cross-cultural differences and gender. Furthermore, most research on leadership is drawn from observation and study of men in leadership roles and as a result, women often question its validity for women in leadership roles.

Mary Parker Follet

Mary Parker Follett, was an American political scientist and management thinker who was well known in the 1920s on both sides of the Atlantic, but whose ideas became hidden from history during and after the Second World War. This was largely because of her conceptualization of *power with* rather than *power over* others as the key to social progress and business success.

She was and remains a key contributor to the development of leadership thinking. There are commentaries reflecting on the contemporary relevance of her work by John Child, Nitin Nohria, Warren Bennis, Henry Mintzberg, Angela Dumas, Tokihiko Enomoto and Sir Peter Parker, together with a preface by Ros Moss Kanter, an epilogue by Paul R. Lawrence and a substantial chapter, "Mary Parker Follett: a Pioneering Life," by Pauline Graham.

The fact that so many distinguished writers, in the past and today, have given credit to her contribution demonstrates a sound belief in what she has to say.

Mary Parker Follett's philosophical teachings encompass far more than how to run a successful business organization. Anyone who reads the book, *Mary Parker Follett – Prophet of Management: a Celebration of Writings from the 1920*, will have to re-think leadership, and think holistically and with integrity about the nature and practice of democratic governance in human society, of which the business organization is a microcosm.

Warren Bennis

Bennis is one of the founding fathers of leadership and change theories. His first book, entitled *The Planning of Change*, was written in 1962, and he is today a professor of management at the University of California and an author of many books on leadership and change including the book, *On Becoming A Leader*.

John Kotter

John Kotter is one of the best known writers on the subject of change, in particular, organizational change. However, his real specialism is in the area of leadership. In his book *Leading Change*, John Kotter examines the efforts of more than 100 companies to remake themselves into better competitors. He identifies the most common mistakes and he offers eight steps to overcoming obstacles and for successfully implementing change.

Daryl Conner

Conner founded possibly the first change consulting company in the 1970s, and developed the Organizational Development Resources methodology that is widely used in many management consultancy firms and in first-class organizations. He has written many books on the subject of change and leadership.

Jeannie Daniel Duck

Ms Duck is the vice-president of The Boston Consulting Group, and she carries a battle-bloodied authority about the subject of leading change. Her "change curve model" has five phases.

» **Stagnation**: when the need for change shows up in data or performance.
» **Preparation**: when the decision to change is made and an outline of the strategy developed.
» **Implementation**: when the plan swings into action.

» **Determination**: when the decision is made for an organization to retreat or to go ahead.
» **Fruition**: when it all pays off.

Her latest book is titled *The Change Monster: Forces That Fuel or Foil Corporate Transformation and Change*.

Kurt Lewin's change model

This is the famous change model which is the theoretical foundation upon which change theory is built. This widely known and much used model has three stages: unfreezing, changing, and refreezing.

Lewin said that we cannot understand an organization without trying to change it; therefore, I conclude that leaders cannot therefore make an adequate diagnosis without intervening. Lewin points out that the change process is an integrated one and we cannot keep it all separate. The gravest mistake a change leader can make is to attempt to "separate the notion of diagnosis from the notion of intervention."

Donald Schon and Chris Argris

Theirs is the concept of the change leader as a reflective practitioner. Thoreau taught: "How can we remember our ignorance, which our growth requires, when we are using our knowledge all the time?"

Donald Schon has provided an individual, self-directed, experience-based professional learning and developmental process for the practitioner with the concept of the *reflective practitioner*.

The truly reflective practitioner, says Schon (1991), actively participates in this molding of the social order through "praxis" (this means informed, directed and committed action) but not all professionals embrace the same level of reflective activity and commitment to action. In a fast-changing society in which the direction for change cannot be predicted, the ability to critically analyze, make informed judgments and direct actions, would be very much valued.

Charles Handy

Handy has had an interesting influence on organizational thinking, particularly in the area of organizational *culture*. His four cultures, adapted from the work of Harrison, are very easy for people to understand and groups readily identify with them and begin to explore their culture through the models he uses. According to Handy, there are four cultures: the power culture, the role culture, the task culture, and the person culture.

Henri Fayol (1841–1925)

Fayol was a French engineer whose key contribution to the leadership development was his work *Administration Industrielle et Generale* written in 1916. Fayol belongs to the classical school of management theory and was particularly interested in authority and its implementation. He advocated a consistent set of principles that all organizations need to run properly.

Until today, his *five functions* still form the basis of much of modern management thought and action.

1 Plan (and look ahead)
2 Organize
3 Command
4 Co-ordinate
5 Control (feedback and inspect)

Alan Hooper and John Potter

Co-authors of the book *Intelligent Leadership* and famous for their work on the competencies of leadership and on the concept of the "learning leader."

Abraham Maslow

Hierarchy of need. This is a much used concept and a very powerful one too with regard to leading change. Indeed it is pertinent to the whole business of living and relating to others. In my experience I have learnt, sometimes painfully, how even those changes that are meant to be for the *greater good* can come crashing down like Humpty Dumpty if people think that their basic needs are threatened in any way. This is because of the critical importance of security to human beings. At the end of the day, the bottom-line question is, "how is this going to affect me?" The hierarchy of need pyramid addresses these basic needs:

» Physiological
» Security
» Social
» Status
» Self Fulfillment.

Rosabeth Moss Kanter

Her main concepts include:

» managing resistance to change
» empowerment
» bureaucracy
» changing organizations.

Moss Kanter proposes that change masters are people and organizations adept at the art of anticipating the need for productive change, and of leading it. She identifies innovation, entrepreneurship and the development of participative management skills as the key to corporate renaissance. Furthermore, she advocates participative management and empowerment and best use of people, the need for synergy in organizations, flatter structures, more responsive leaders, partnerships and collaboration.

NOTES

1 Franchini, N. (1999) "What's the story?" *Professional Manager*, **8**(5) September.
2 Hooper, A. & Potter, J. (2000) *Intelligent Leadership*. Random House Business, London.

A Guide To Useful Resources

A brief summary of books, articles, and useful websites on leadership and change.

"Discovery consists in seeing what everyone else has seen, but thinking what no one else has."

Albert Szent-Gyorgyi

The following is a wide range of information and reading on the subject of leadership and change. It includes books, journals and periodicals, as well as informative websites.

BOOKS AND ARTICLES

Adair, J. (1983) *Effective Leadership*. Gower Press, London.

Adair, J. (1997) *Not Bosses But Leaders*. Talbot Adair Press, London.

Argyris, C. (1992) *On Organisational Learning*. Blackwell Publishers, Cambridge, MA.

Argyris, C. & Schon, D.A. (1974) *Theory in Practice: Increasing professional effectiveness*. Jossey-Bass, San Francisco.

Argyris, C., Schon, D. & Payne, M. (eds) (1996) *Organizational Learning II: Theory, Method, and Practice*, Addison-Wesley Series on Organizational Development. Addison-Wesley, Reading, MA.

Axelrod, R. & Cohen, M.D. (2000) *Harnessing complexity: organizational implications of a scientific frontier*. Simon & Schuster, New York.

Bartlett, C.A. & Ghoshal, S. (1989) The Transnational Organisation [from "Managing across borders: new organizational responses." *Sloane Management Review* ((1987)) fall, pp. 43–53].

Basu, R. (2001) "Measuring e-business performance: a prescription for the pharmaceutical industry." *Professional Consultancy*, issue 001 (June).

Bennis, W. (1990) *On Becoming a Leader*. Hutchinson Business Books, London.

Berry, L. (1999) "Discovering the Soul of Service." *Customer Service Management*, issue XXV (May/June).

Boston, B.O. (1972) "Paulo Freire: Notes of a loving critic." In Grabowski, S. (ed.), *Paulo Freire: A Revolutionary Dilemma for the Adult Educator*. Publications in Continuing Education, Syracuse, NY; available from the ERIC Clearhouse in Adult Education.

Boud, D., Keogh, R. & Walker, D. (eds) (1985) *Reflection: Turning Experience into Learning*. Kogan Page, London.

Bowon, K. & Yoonseok, L. (2001) "Global capacity expansion strategies: lessons learned from two Korean carmakers." *Long Range Planning*, **34**.

Brown, M. (1988) *The Dinosaur Strain – The Survivor's Guide to Personal and Business Success*. Sound Thinking, London.

Bruce, A. (1998) "Aiming for change – stay on target." *Professional Manager*, **7**(5).

Bunning, C. (1991) "Turning experience into learning: the strategic challenge for individuals and organisations." *Training & Development in Australia*, **18**(4) (December).

Casey, D. (1985) "The awful nature of change." *Management Education and Development*, **16**(1).

Conner, D. (1998) *Leading at the Edge of Chaos: How to Create the Nimble Organization*. John Wiley & Sons, New York.

Conner, D.R. (1994) "Bouncing back." *Sky Magazine*, Delta Airlines, September.

Couldwell, C. (2001) "Everybody's dropping 'e'." *Business Solutions, The Evening Standard*, Tuesday June 12.

Covey, S.R. (1992) *The Seven Habits of Highly Effective People*. Simon & Schuster, London.

Crainer, S. (1996) "Bridging the gap between noble aspirations and reality." *Professional Manager*, **5**(4) (July).

Dess, G.G., Picken, J.C. & Lyon, D.W. (1998) "Transformational leadership: lessons from U.S. experience." *Long Range Planning, International Journal of Strategic Management*, **31**(5) (October – The Strategic Planning Society).

Drucker, P.F. (1989) *The Practice of Management*. p. 156. Heinemann Professional, London.

Elliot, R.D. (1990) "The challenge of managing change." *Personnel Journal*, **69**(3) (March), 6–9.

English, P. et al. (2001) "Your guide to e-learning." *Personnel Today*, April 3.

Fenton, J. (1988) *101 Ways To Boost Your Business Performance*. Heinemann Publishing, London.

Fromm, E. (1988) *The Art of Loving*. Unwin Hyman, London.

Gass, B. (2000) *Word for Today*. UCB Press, Dublin.

Goleman, D. (1995) *Emotional Intelligence*. Bantam Books, New York.

Graham, P. (ed.) (1995) *Mary Parker Follett – Prophet of Management: a Celebration of Writings from the 1920s* (a Harvard Business School Press Classic). Harvard Business School Press, Boston, MA. Reviewed by Dr Mary King, FRSA (former lecturer in Industrial Technology and in Women's Studies at Bradford).

Guillevic, E. (1969) *Selected Poems*, tr. Denise Levertov. New Directions, New York.

Handy, C. (1991) *The Age Of Unreason*. Arrow Books, London.

Handy, C. (1993) *Understanding Organisations*. Penguin Books, London.

Harrison, N. (2000) *Improving Employee Performance, a Sunday Times*/Kogan Page publication. Kogan Page, London.

Harvard Business Review (1998) *Harvard Business Review on Change*, Harvard Business Review series. Harvard Business School Press, Boston, MA.

Harvey, D. (2001) *Creating The Collaborative Business*, a Business Intelligence White Paper. Business Intelligence, London.

Heller, R (2001) *Stephen Covey*. Dorling Kindersley, London.

Hinterhuber, H.H. & Krauthammer, E. (1997) "The leadership heel." *Strategy Magazine*, (August/September).

Holec, J., Miller, F.D. & Redwood, S. (1993) *Companies without Boundaries: Planning and Implementing the Global Future*, a PricewaterhouseCoopers publication. Penguin, London.

Hooper, A. & Potter, J. (2000) *Intelligent Leadership*. Random House Business, London.

Institute of Directors, London (1998) *Sign of the Times*. Institute of Directors, London.

Katzenbach, J. *et al.* (1997) "The myth of the top management team." *Harvard Business Review*, (November/December).

Katzenbach, J. *et al.* (1997) *Real Change Leaders*. Nicholas Brealey Publishing, London.

Kennedy C. (2001) "The roadmap to success: how Gerhard Schumeyer changed the culture at Siemens Nixdorf." *Long Range Planning, International Journal of Strategic Management*, **31**(February), 262–271.

Koch, R. (1997) *The 80-20 Principle*. Nicholas Brealey Publishing, London.

Kopp, S. (1974) *If You Meet the Buddha on the Road, Kill Him*. Sheldon Press, London.

Kotter, J. (1996) *Leading Change*. Harvard Business School Press, Boston, MA.

Lewin, K. (1935) *A dynamic theory of personality*. McGraw-Hill, New York.

Lieber, R. (2001) "Information is everything." *Fast Company*, **29**, 247.

Management Today (1997) *What Price Reputation*, Report. Haymarket Publishing, London.

Meikeljohn, I. (2001) "Putting intelligence back into business." *Business Solutions, The Evening Standard*, Tuesday June 12.

Mezias, J.M., Grinyer, P. & Guth, W.D. (2001) "Changing collective cognition: a process model for strategic change." *Long Range Planning, International Journal of Strategic Management*, **34** (February), 72.

Mezirow, J. (1978) *Perspective Transformation*. Adult Education, London.

Morgan, G. (1997) *Images of Organisation*. Sage Publications, London.

Moss Kanter, R. (1988) *Change Masters*. Allen & Unwin, London.

Moss Kanter, R. (2001) *Evolve*. Harvard Business School Press, Boston, MA.

Mullins, L.J. (1985) *Management and Organisational Behaviour*, 4th edn. Pitman Publishing, London.

Northern College (1998) *Handbook of MSc in Advanced Professional Studies*. Northern College of Education, Dundee.

O'Connor, C.A. (1993) *The Handbook for Organisational Change*, The McGraw-Hill Training Series. McGraw-Hill Book Company Europe, London.

Perren, L. & Tavakoli, I. (1997) "Mission impossible without commitment." *Professional Manager*, **6**(4) (July).

Peters, T.J. & Waterman Jr, R.H. (1995) *In Search of Excellence*. HarperCollins Business, New York.

PriceWaterhouseCoopers Change Integration Team, The (1995) *Better Change*. Irwin Professional Publishing, New York.

Reich, R.B. (2001) "Your job is change." *Fast Company*, issue 39, 140.

Roddick, A. (1991) *Body and Soul*, p. 214. Ebury Press, London.

Ryback, D. (1998) *Putting Emotional Intelligence to Work: Successful Leadership Is More Than IQ*. Butterworth-Heinneman, London.

Scholes, E. & Clutterbuck, D. (2001) "Communication with stakeholders: an integrated approach." *Long Range Planning, International Journal of Strategic Management*, **31**(February), 72.

Schon, D. (1971) *Beyond the Stable State*. Hutchinson, London.

Schruijer, S. & Vasina, L. (eds) (1999) "Leadership and organizational change: an introduction." *European Journal of Work and Organizational Psychology*, **8**(1) (March).

Senge, P., Kleiner, A., Roberts, C., Ross, R., Roth, G. & Smith, B. (1999) *The Dance of Change*. Nicholas Brealey Publishing, London.

Sharman, C. (1997) "Looking for tomorrow's leaders." *Management Today* (August).

Slater, R. (2000) *The GE Way Fieldbook*. McGraw Hill, New York.

Tapscott D. (1996) *The Digital Economy*. McGraw Hill, New York.

Tosi Jr, H.L. & Slocum Jr, J.W. (1984) "Contingency theory: some suggested directions." *Journal of Management*, **10**(1).

Warner Weil, S. & McGill, I. (1989) *Making Sense of Experiential Learning*. SRHE and Open University Press, London.

Watson, C.M. (1983) "Leadership, management and the seven keys." *Business Horizons* (March–April), 8–13.

Wheatley, R. & Parker, N. (1995) *Empowerment/Self-directed Work Teams*. Institute of Management, London.

Williamson, M. (1996) *A Return to Love*. HarperCollins, New York.

RELEVANT BOOKS' WEBSITES

www.LeadershipAndChangeBooks.com
www.InternetEconomyBooks.com
www.KnowledgeAndLearningBooks.com
www.StrategyAndCompetitionBooks.com
www.Human-Resource-Management-Books.com
www.DigitalEnterpriseBooks.com

LEADERSHIP AND CHANGE LINKS

http://www.cranfield.ac.uk/som/
  Cranfield University – Cranfield School of Management
http://www.economist.co.uk/
  The Economist
http://www.fortune.com/
  Fortune Magazine
http://www.fastcompany.com/home.html/
  fastcompany.com
http://www.hbsp.harvard.edu/products/press/books/kotter.html
  Harvard Business School Publishing
http://www.hbsp.harvard.edu/products/hbr/index.html
  Harvard Business Review
http://www.eurosite.de/
  Human Performance Improvement
http://web.idirect.com/~vfr/archives3.html
  The CEO Refresher Archives
http://www.refresher.com/!leadingchange
http://www.csmintl.premierdomain.com/leading_strategic_
  change.htm
  Center for Strategic Management
http://arl.cni.org/newsltr/191/inst.html
  OMS Institute on Leading Change
http://www.meansbusiness.com/Leadership-and-Change-Books.htm
  meanbusiness (leadership and change books)
  Organisations & Consultancy @OnePine
http://www.onepine.demon.co.uk/lead1.htm

JOURNALS AND PERIODICALS

Academy of Management Journal
Californian Management Review
Journal of Change Management
Journal of Management Consultants
Journal of Strategic Change

Long Range Planning (The Strategic Planning Society)
Management Review
McKinsey Quarterly
Sloan Management Review
Fast Company

Leading Change – Making it Work

Guidance on how to lead sustainable, fundamental and successful change. An insight into how organizations can inform and invent their futures; and the role of leadership in an ever-changing world.

''We are always teaching; we are always learning; we are always changing.''

(unknown)

Many change management programs fail because they do not appreciate and value the synthesis between the mechanical and human components of change.

Effective change leaders work from where they are instead of working from the top; and they co-build communities of leaders and centers of excellence. In the world of dinosaurs, leaders tend to depend on title, authority, or official sanction to undertake their change programs. But the truth is that no one person can possess all the leadership characteristics and it is unlikely that the people at the top can know enough about technology, markets, or the potential of people in and around the organization to be the major instigators of change. There's no way that change can be planned as a formal ''program.'' The job of those people leading change is to create an environment in which change insurgency can flourish.

Also, some change initiatives fail because the change process does not address the leader's need to coach others through the transition process; and they do not acknowledge the need for leaders themselves to be coached before they can effectively lead and coach others. There is a good illustration in Zechariah Chapter 13 v 7 ''If the shepherd is smitten the sheep will be scattered.''

There is a delightful book by Marian Zimmer Bradley called the *Mists of Avalon*. The mists of Avalon are a mythical allusion to the tales of King Arthur. Avalon is a magical island that is hidden behind huge impenetrable mists. Until the mists part, there is no way to navigate your way to the island. *But unless you believe that the island is there, the mists won't part*. The mists part when we believe that Avalon is behind them. And that is what success to effective change leadership is: a parting of the mists, a shift in perception, in attitudes, in behavior, in mindsets.

BEGIN WITH THE END IN SIGHT

''What the wise do in the beginning, fools do in the end.''

Warren Buffet

In this section, I shall be talking about goals setting and planning by a process which Steven Covey describes a mental creation. Some writers and practitioners call it mind mapping.

My model (PLANE) is illustrated below and handy hints are suggested for change leaders piloting unchartered skies.

THE PLANE MODEL

» **Plan**: to prepare, including vision; strategy to achieve vision; time; people (roles and responsibilities); place; resources; scheme of arrangement; communication plan; performance measures to validate the value of the change initiative; benefits to be realized; enablers; and contingencies. *First, create a vision.* In the words of Lewis Carroll, the novelist: "If you do not know where you are going, then any road will take you there."

» **Learn**: acquire knowledge of area of activity; gain awareness of information from observation; receive instruction for veterans of change; equip yourself with the knowledge, wisdom and understanding needed for the journey; and share with the all participants in the change initiative and relatives (cross-discipline).

» **Armament**: equip and mobilize your people with the necessary resources. Resources include facilities, equipment, materials, budget, knowledge, support mechanisms, education and training. This should also include an assessment of the total resource commitment (cost) and an estimation of the duration of the change initiative, including tasks.

» **Navigate**: indicate route and manage direct course. This involves taking overall responsibility for the change initiative but ensuring that all participants are responsible for one thing or the other. Admiral Rickover once said: "Responsibility is a unique concept. When you share it, your portion is not diminished. When you delegate it, it is still with you. No amount of ignorance or 'passing the buck' can shift it. Unless someone can point their finger at you when something goes wrong, then the truth is, you were never responsible to begin with."

> » **Evaluate:** assess performance and the benefits realized from the change initiatives; lessons learnt (both negative and positive); re-fuel; re-charge; re-visit strategy and original change plan; plan.

Every successful leader knows that the business strategy must be an evolving one. We need goals to aim for, but a highly organized *"change"* plan dictated by reason and logic is bound to get derailed eventually. The future is too unpredictable. By locking the door against any future we restrict ourselves, as leaders, and our organizations intolerably. How can leaders be used to play an exciting part if they just see the organizations as a big mess and refuse to come out of their immaculate well-ordered shell?

Thus leading change is about embracing the chaos and living dynamically.

Successful change ultimately depends upon the ability to manage people, ideas and resources simultaneously. Each area is equally crucial.

Change is a cyclical process, you can never improve enough and the future is unpredictable.

CREATE A SENSE OF URGENCY

"Urgency does not equal fear. Fear hurts, urgency helps."
(unknown)

Although creating a sense of urgency should be pretty straightforward, John Kotter of Harvard University maintains, based on a study of more than 100 companies, that it is not. This is the phase where the change initiative threatens to collapse before it has even started. This can be attributed to the fact that some leaders tend to underestimate the effort that is needed to move people from their comfort zone into a *new state*. They also tend to overestimate their rate of success in communicating a sense of urgency.

Enough time cannot be spent on this phase and this is a key point because some leaders' senior executives start to become nonchalant about the mobilization effort after a while and think: "well, they should be motivated enough by now. This is the end of the second week of business engagement and mobilization!"

But leaders have to be patient and the momentum has to be kept up. One to three weeks without activity and visibility causes the change initiative to flounder. In addition to mobilizing the forces, this phase also includes examination of the market and competitive realities; and the development of contingency plans for potential pitfalls; and the means for identifying opportunities.

It is important to say here that business engagement and mobilization require great leaders and change champions, because this phase is the uphill push – where there needs to be sufficient motivation and sustained effort to see the change initiative through successfully.

Creating a sense of urgency

» Electrify your vision! Vision statements become electrified when you set milestones.
» Don't wait for motivation! Start, and motivation will come.
» Develop superb communication of the vision and the case for change – this communication must address how others think, feel, and act.
» Communicate a clear sense of direction.
» Create a high sense of urgency within the managerial rank to put a guiding coalition together; and provide robust support mechanisms.
» Plan for and create *"quick wins"* to sustain the momentum.
» Publicly declare early successes.
» Communicate clearly and frequently, especially about measurements, results and consequences.
» Get the whole organization together on occasions – this can build momentum, create a memorable event, and build healthy peer pressure for change.

In their article, "Transformational leadership: lessons from U.S. experience",[1] Dess, Picken and Lyon commented that "it does little good for the troops to believe they are up to their ass in alligators, unless they are also confident their leader knows the way out of the swamp!"

IGNITE THE COLLECTIVE WILL

"There are few, if any jobs in which ability alone is sufficient. Needed also, are loyalty, sincerity, enthusiasm, and team play."

William B. Given, Jr

Transparency of the leader's contributions

The leader who makes clear his intention to participate in the change initiative and coherently communicates his part will be able to engage the workforce. A significant number of change initiatives fail because leadership expects the workforce to do all the work. An effective change leader has to take his or her people through changes that they may find unsettling and therefore cannot be passive. Leaders of change should also share the dangers and the hardships of their people.

A major part of good change leadership is the leader's relationship with those being led and his or her attitude towards them. This will determine how they see their roles in the change initiative. If the there is no relationship or the relationship is not good, they might see themselves as: "the unwilling, led by the unknown, achieving the impossible for the ungrateful"

The change leader needs to build a meaningful relationship with the people and this involves a significant investment in his or her personal learning in conjunction with learning about the individuals and the organization as a whole. People are governed by their emotions rather than their intellect and successful change leaders are those who can persuade others to follow them. It is a personal thing.

It is not that people usually lack the strength to effect change; it is the will that can be missing. Len Berry said: "Hard work is not what defeats most people on the job. What defeats them is work without personal growth, without team-mates, without kindness, without meaning; companies that care only about making money are destined for mediocrity, if not outright failure, because sustaining service performance requires encouraging employees' hearts; a goal of making money in and of itself is not heartening."

Community development

Ironically, I have been faced with progressive leaders of change who espouse the democratic process of change but turn round to suggest:

"Get on with the job." My position has always been to highlight the fatal deficiency of this approach because I believe that it is essential for leadership to be engaged in the change process and to be active participants. I believe that, especially in these days of massive changes, it is not realistic to expect that just one person can lead the scale of changes required in this environment. Hence, it is important for the change leaders to build communities of practice that can enable the change initiatives to succeed.

Role modeling

Visionary leaders of change have got to be role models and set a positive example if they wish to influence the behavior of those they simultaneously lead and serve. Effective change leaders are "walking missionaries" in their organizations – they constantly demonstrate and express in day-to-day activities their preferred ways of doing business. Employees are left in no doubt about the way things should be done. Real change leaders create the cultural values and rules that guide the organization in the choice of strategy, decision parameters and behavior standards. To implement and sustain successful and fundamental change, leadership has to be seen – and it is best seen in action. Words paint pictures – people need to see it as well as hear it.

Creativity

Leaders should encourage creativity and unleash the creative forces within their companies. They should create an atrium for curiosity, exploration and experience. It is the change leader's role to stimulate and encourage creativity by providing the conditions and resources for its healthy growth and development.

Empowerment

Current experience indicates that if the needs and motivation of the workforce are satisfactorily aligned to the agreed purposes of the organization, then effectiveness and efficiency are likely outcomes. The evidence from a detailed study of well-run companies is that long-term profitability is best achieved where management processes are built around personal empowerment and active involvement of all workers.

"Come to edge," he said.
They said, "We are afraid."
"Come to the edge," he said.
They came.
And he pushed them.
And they flew.

Guillaume Apollinaire

COMMITMENT TO EXCELLENCE

"Excellence requires 100% all the time. If you doubt that, try maintaining excellence by setting standards of 92% or even 95%. Pretty soon you will feel fine as long as you get near it. When that happens, excellence gets reduced to ACCEPTABLE and acceptable does not seem worth it if you can get by with ADEQUATE. After that MEDIOCRITY is only a breath away."

Chuck Swindoll

In the latest edition of the Collins English Dictionary, "excellence" is described as *"the state or quality of excelling or being exceptionally good."*

It is essential that that leaders promote the adoption of best practice and the drive for business excellence throughout their organizations. I am referring to the need to begin benchmarking internally and externally; and learning from the best. One cannot over-emphasize the importance of achieving competitive advantage regardless of the size of the business. It is no longer sufficient to be just good enough. In terms of business performance, huge savings in one area become rather academic if they are outweighed by wastage in another area. Therefore, organizations need to be committed to excellence in all areas of the business: people, processes, technology, and systems.

This calls for the leaders to take a robustly holistic and outward-looking approach to excellence. Externally, leaders have to look to their competitors around the globe and to leading businesses in other sectors in order to learn best practices for success. Internally, leaders have to look to successful leaders of change for inspiration and wisdom; as well as look to the gems in their workforce as co-builders of a culture of excellence.

"JDI" (Just Do It) is now part of the business language. It is not uncommon to see leadership throw money at projects and tell the people to get on with it. Not surprisingly, most if not all of those "JDI" projects fail because no one at the top is interested in them. "JDI" works only when people are equipped for the change process. It does not work and in fact does a lot of damage when people are thrown into the change process blindfolded and with hands bound. Many leaders have learnt the painful lesson that average doesn't look so good when you realize that it is just the worst of the best and the best of the worst.

In recent years, a lot of thought has gone into what we now call "organizational excellence." Leaders of first-rate organizations are beginning to realize that it is not enough to survive and it is not enough to grow: organizations have to grow better and become more effective. Apart from financial measurements of success such as profits and sales, there are other factors that are involved in creating *excellence*. And these are the softer issues of people, values, motivation, empowerment and satisfaction (for employees, customers, partners, shareholders and other stakeholders). Tom Peters and Robert Waterman triggered this shift in their book *In Search of Excellence*. Excellence, however, starts from the top, from leadership. A well known saying is "the fish rots from the head" – if leadership is not committed to excellence, and is not committed to fundamentally changing collective cognition and the resultant organizational behavior required for the change initiative to succeed, it labors only but in vain.

The hallmarks of excellence embrace the ten ways listed in this chapter for leading change effectively and I add, excellence is underpinned by sound, personalized, organizational values. Walter Goldsmith and David Clutterbuck came up with a set of factors they, and I, believe distinguishes excellent companies from the rest. I have adapted this to reflect my thinking, based on experience.

SYMBOLS OF EXCELLENCE

1 A rigorous, not rigid, corporate strategy, which incorporates clear measurement systems (with both internal and external focus).

2 Leadership's belief, visibility, involvement and commitment.

3 Autonomy, initiative and creativity.

4 Situational leadership and appropriate use of controls.

5 Effective governance.

6 Involvement of stakeholders and effective communication.

7 Market focus – strong ability to anticipate markets and strong business focus.

8 Commitment to excellence in all things, great and small. This involves instilling pride and ownership in the workforce.

9 Robust measurement systems around the desired changes and frequent reports of results.

10 A culture where employees can say, "I am the organisation."

11 Innovation and creativity – leaders should create mild forms of instability in order to stimulate change and continuous improvement in performance. As John Kao, of *Jamming*, said, "today's business is seeking another advantage – creative advantage."

12 Integrity.

13 Fun.

Excellence is closely linked to decisiveness. I once worked on a major business transformation program, which was eventually canned after a few million pounds had been invested in it. The problem was that there was no clear business strategy and the leadership was weak. Once when I was discussing the program with a colleague who had not worked on the project but who knew the change leader, he (my colleague) remarked: "But he (the change leader) is such a nice guy." I tersely replied: "In that particular situation, he could not afford to be *simply* a 'Mr. Nice Guy.' We all want to be liked, but at some point you have got to ask yourself how much you are willing to lose in order to be accepted. Furthermore, sometimes the decision to do nothing is wise, but you can't make a career out of it!"

This reminds me of a story I was told. Freddy Fulcrum weighed up everything too carefully. He would say: "On the one hand . . . but then . . . on the other." His arguments weighed out so evenly that he never did anything. When Freddy finally died, they carved a big zero on his tombstone!

Some leaders prattle on till they become all things to all men and women – and no one is sure of what they stand for.

I admit it may not be feasible for an organization to achieve all the above but I believe that if you always meet your expectations, they probably were never high enough in the first place. At the end of the day, only those who risk going too far can possibly find out how far one can go.

THE LEADER AS A LEARNER

"Everybody thinks of changing humanity and nobody thinks of changing himself."

Leo Tolstoy

We have moved beyond the stable state – change is proceeding at an exponential rate and has become increasingly pervasive. Donald Schon (1971) said:

"the loss of the stable state means that our society and all of its institutions are in a continuing process of transformation. Therefore, it becomes imperative for the leader to become adept at learning to understand, guide, influence and manage these transformations. Leaders must be able not only to transform our organizations, in response to changing situations and require-ments; we must invent and develop organizations that are 'learning systems', that is to say, systems capable of bringing about their continual transformation."[2]

In *Management Today*, August 1997, Colin Sharman, then UK senior partner for KPMG, wrote:

"Leaders must be learners and your people must believe that you know at least as much as they do about the change initia-tive – mercifully, more than they do."[3]

Gaining qualifications is just the start of learning: the pace of change means that learning has to be a lifelong activity. Intention does not equal effect. This learning includes learning to be readers of situations;

interpreters of situations; and authors of situations. In essence, while the required change of empowered individuals in the organization is significant, an even greater change is required in the behavior of the change leader.

The pace of change demands that leaders of change have got to be lifelong learners. They have to keep abreast of developments in their own field and related fields of activity; and they need to understand the trends in the business world. Learning gives breadth of perspective; increases the ability to understand the bigger picture; and equips the mind to dare to progress into the unknown. After all, the *unknown* is simply the *untried*. Learning is a personal responsibility and its pursuit is a mind-set.

Insufficient learning leads to the proposition which Reg Revans calls the Principle of Insufficient Mandate: "Leaders who cannot change their own perceptions of their problems [because of lack of knowledge – my addition] cannot change the conditions that create these problems." Or: "Without authority over one's opinions one has no authority over one's surroundings."

In order to overcome the learning disability that can impair leadership effectiveness and success, the leader has first got to know himself or herself. This refers to the Delphic motto: Know Thyself, and is the mainspring of all psychology. A good leader should ask: "Am I part of that which I seek to change?"

A good leader will recognize what he or she does not know, and would be willing to invest in continuous learning. Good leaders also recognize their shortcomings and seek to find and work with others who are strong in those areas where they are weak.

The challenge is to narrow the gap between the sense of integration between our learning (that is, what we have learnt) and our actual transactions with our internal and external stakeholders.

In addition to the personal learning and development, change leaders have got to be commercially astute and bring the market-place realities more clearly into focus and on to the agenda. They need to get better at seeking and providing internal feedback as well as a more accurate and compelling case for change from both the internal and the external perspectives. This is to say they have to know their field of activity and do their homework thoroughly by building a track record of knowing where the next big impact is going to be; and by anticipating the markets.

Lastly, we must remember that excellence and learning are interwoven. Kolb (1984) speaks of learning "as the process whereby knowledge is created through the transformation of experience." His cycle addresses learning as a dialectic between "grasping" what is happening on concrete and abstract levels, and actively and rapidly transforming such experience – through reflection or observation, and the testing or application of learning outcomes – into practice. Few organizations, in my experience, go back to review their change initiatives in order to assess where they got stuck. If the initiative was eventually successful, they move forward in euphoria, losing valuable lessons in the process. If the initiative was a failure, they get trapped into the "Wasn't that just awful?" mode and move on to the next change cycle leaving loose threads and uncaptured lessons behind. Consequently, the same old mistakes get repeated over and over again because there was no diagnosis, and no prescription.

Effective change leaders ensure that lessons learnt are captured and transformed into organizational learning.

To conclude, Ernest Hemingway remarked one time that "nobody knows what's in him until he tries to pull it out. If there's nothing or very little, the shock can kill a man."

IDENTIFY AND MANAGE RESISTANCE TO CHANGE

"Nothing will ever be attempted, if all possible objections must first be overcome."

Samuel Johnson

Resistance, subtle or obvious, is a slow-motion response to meet agreements to change, or even a complete refusal to cooperate with change. Some of the people I have spoken to lately see *resistance to change* as one of the perks of their jobs, actually as a given in their job descriptions. Why? This is because they are change weary and suspicious of the rhetoric spewed forth by leaders. The leaders who are flexible and adaptable themselves are able to deal effectively with resistance to change. This issue of resistance to change far outweighs any other aspect of the change process, whether it is visioning, planning the change, evaluation or leadership issues. Figure 10.1 illustrates the point as Moses leads the children of Israel through the Red Sea.

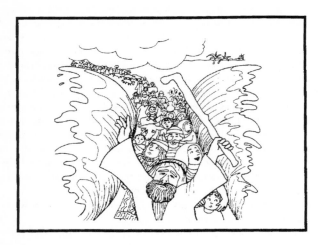

'All right, stop right there...who just said...

"it's a bit muddy, isn't it?..."'

Unknown

Fig. 10.1 Moses leads the children of Israel through the Red Sea.

Leaders who aim to achieve fundamental and sustainable change cannot afford to neglect the dynamics of personal and organizational transition that can determine the outcome of any change effort.

In years gone by, leaders could simply order changes to happen and wait for the outcomes, favorable or not. Even today, in some corridors of power, many leaders still view the delivery of transformation and/or change as a straightforward, linear process, largely *soul-less*: determine what needs to be done (establish tasks), timescales, roles and responsibility. Then all that seems left for the organization is to implement the plan and to adapt. So, why don't they just do it?

Change is a complex, psychological event. Even when we analyze the business processes and systems and re-engineer and/or reorganize, people's reactions will prove decisive to the success or failure of the initiative. The power of change needs to be respected and managed for the word "change" usually means different things to different people.

I like Gareth Morgan's use of the "pig" metaphor in his book, *Imaginization*. His question: what is a pig? It appears to be a simple question at first, but the answer is not as simple because a pig is many things to different people. For the wolf, the pig is food; for the Muslim, it is an unclean animal; for the butcher and the farmer the pig is a commercial item; the veterinarian is interested in the state of health of the pig; the child sees the pig as a pet and thinks of the story of the three little pigs; and so on.

For example, to the chief executive, "change" means displaying leadership by developing a vision of the future, developing strategies to bring that vision into reality and then managing the crises that arises on the journey. It is also about political warfare and winning the battles to ensure that everybody in the organization is mobilized towards the same goals and objectives. This is what Alan Hooper and John Potter call "emotional alignment."

To the production line worker, the salesperson and the truck driver, change frequently is perceived to be a threat to the *status quo*.

Therefore, the precise meaning and significance of "change" will vary according to the frame of reference through which it is viewed. Each frame opens or closes a horizon of understanding by directing attention in a particular way. Perceptions of what the change involves and the implications for the business and staff personally need to be identified and managed.

In order to do this, leaders should recognize the distinction between their world and that of those around them, including those lower in the organization. Managing effective change does not allow for dealing with a single reality: there is not just one bottom line! It involves managing multiple realities as seen through various people's lenses – their fears, their anxieties, their hopes, their aspirations, their views. This is why more and more often you find that when you ask any good management consultant or guru a *"How to"* question, they say *"Well, it all depends."* Contingency theory rules supreme. This is the difficulty with the science of management whose central quest is to produce a set of *general rules*.

It is difficult because organizations are unique and our times are without precedent. As Aladdin sang in the Disney movie, *"It's a whole new world."*

The task for change leaders is to learn to skillfully read, interpret and to swiftly act as a Dyno-Rod, which is to unblock the drains and to act as a catalyst (with other change insurgents) to identify the organization's defensive routines; and learn how to overcome them.

There are various reasons why people resist change and they include the following.

» Leadership has not articulately communicated the reason for the change – there is no "story."
» The employees think that the leaders have got it wrong! That their analysis, data and strategy is wrong. (*"What does he know about what we do in our department?" "How can he understand when he is so remote from the coal face?"*)
» The employees think that the change would harm their self-interest.
» Their implicit and explicit theories of cause and effect differ from the leader's and thus their predictions about the speed of change and about the effect of the change initiative also differ.
» With technology-driven change initiatives, there are fears of the automation of roles.

Managing resistance to change

» Leaders should expect resistance to change.
» *"Seek first to understand, and then to be understood"* – leaders should seek to understand the driving forces behind resistance to change, in particular the personal and emotional issues.
» They should also send out clear signals that open resistance would be rewarded and should build robust feedback mechanisms and processes.
» Leaders should endeavor to remove emotive filters when analyzing the resistance because these can distort things. Leaders should view

resistance as fear arising out of lack of ability to do that "*new thing*" or the willingness to do it because "*he does not understand the purpose of doing it and the rationale behind it.*"

» Leaders should create an atrium for expressions of overt resistance and participate in debates.

Even in harmony, you can have struggle and struggle can be positive and productive if managed well. This is what I call the Tartan Principle.

BE RESILIENT

"I don't measure a man's success by how high he climbs, but by how high he bounces when he hits bottom."

General Patton

As one who has led change programs I know that we do not get it right always but we can learn from the experience of the struggle and the mess – and then rise again. However, one has got to get up on the *inside* before one can get up on the *outside*. This takes courage.

One of the authors of *Better Change* (The PriceWaterhouseCoopers Change Integration Team), Ed was once asked what he means by "change management." Upon reflection on his many client assignments over the years, he replied that it really means helping clients to *manage courage*. I can identify with that because I have learnt that it is not because things are difficult that we do not dare; it is because we do not dare that things are difficult.

As the authors of *Better Change* discovered, a deficit of courage is a major impediment to change. Without courage – on the part of the leader of the change initiative – he or she cannot expect to effect the kind or level of positive, significant and fundamental change that is required by today's extremely competitive business environment. Real change leaders identify and boldly open the doors between the *known* and the *unknown*. Some leaders look for the back doors in order to retreat when the chips are down instead of looking for the doors to progress, because they lack the courage to leap over the chasm between success and failure. In their ensuing flight they trip over the bodies of the followers who had believed in their *Moses*.

The thing about courage and valor is that it is subjected to bouts of loneliness. For *uneasy lies the head that wears the crown*. Advancement often brings isolation and criticism but, *"Ya gotta have heart!"* You have got to have the heart and the mind (courage) to do what you've got to do.

Every new level of personal growth leading to success requires a new level of sacrifice. I cannot think of even one person in history who led a life of ease and whose name is worth remembering. If you want to succeed as a leader, you will have to deal with loneliness. The majority will always conform, for that is how you get acceptance. *"But if you want to lead the orchestra, you have got to turn your back on the crowd."* Most successful leaders forge ahead during the time that other people waste – because they have learned how to be alone. Coach Bill Russell of the Bolton Celtics always told his team, "the game is scheduled – we have to pay it; so we might as well win!" If you want to be a successful leader of change, you have got to have the courage to pay the price.

I have the scars to show for my courage. A few weeks ago I met my former boss and mentor, a man I greatly admire. We reminisced about old times and he mentioned some of the difficult times I had whilst leading a major change program in the NHS. I told him that, although it had been painful at the time, the experience went a long way to develop my character and to build resilience in me; also what I learnt in those years, no business school could have taught me or prepared me for.

INJECTING PASSION INTO PRACTICE

"He who knows nothing loves nothing. He who can do nothing understands nothing. He who understands nothing is worthless. But he who understands also loves, notices, sees ... The more knowledge is inherent in a thing, the greater the love ... Anyone who imagines that all fruits ripen at the same time as the strawberries knows nothing about grapes."

Paracelsus

In San Diego's famous *Sea World*, you can actually see ducks on roller skates. Honestly! But when you get close to them you will notice that they do not have their hearts in it. You may smile, but a lot of leaders are like that.

The first and most important attribute of effective change management is the passion to win, to succeed. An effective change leader will (working with others) ensure that people have a clear strategic vision of being the best; and that this is deeply embedded into the psyche of the organization.

In fact, passion and emotion sit at the heart of successful leadership.

Passion becomes evident in the fact that it always implies certain basic elements:

» Care: successful change leaders care about their work. If a woman told us she loved flowers and we saw that she forgot to water them, we would question her "love" for flowers. A good leader looks after his or her initiatives and *waters* them. The essence of caring is to labor for something and 'to make something grow'. Care and labor are inseparable. One cares for that for which one labors, and one labors for that which one cares for.

» Responsibility: care and concern imply another aspect, that of responsibility. To be responsible means to be able and ready to respond. Effective change leaders do not shirk their responsibility and work to generate responsibility in those they lead and work with.

Care and responsibility are mutually interdependent and are essential for a leader to build a meaningful relationship with his or her people; and to influence the people. The truth and the reality is that influence comes from relationships – and this requires a need for the leader to respect and to know his or her people. These attitudes are a syndrome of attitudes which are to be found in a mature leader; that is, the leader who develops his or her own powers productively; who has given up narcissistic dreams of megalomania, omniscience and omnipotence; and who has acquired that rare kind of humility which only genuine productivity can give.

Passion is endearing – it draws people close; it is inspiring – it motivates.

Change leaders must be passionate enough about the strategic goals to ensure victory. The passion must be felt and cascaded throughout the organization so that people have a clear strategic vision of being the best. This should be deeply embedded into the psyche of the organization. The leader must lead the way in communicating the belief that the organization is made up of people and it is not an abstract thing out in space. He or she must arouse those feelings in the followers to the extent that they see themselves as the organization, and as such foster belief in the organization as a champion and contender.

EXPECT SUCCESS

"Im tirtzu eiz zo agada – if you will it, it is no dream."

Theodor Herzl

True change leaders have the passion to win and begin with wild expectations. Expecting something to happen energizes your goal and gives it momentum. There is no room for just trying when leading change – it is either you do or you don't. As George Shultz said: "the minute you start talking about what you are going to do if you lose, you have already lost."

Leaders have to generate a strong element of achievability and communicate this to their employees by, for example:

» having regular walk-arounds
» having regular check-point meetings
» using user/focus groups
» having a dedicated web site to communicate progress and to celebrate success
» having play rooms for new process walk-throughs; familiarization with new technology; brainstorming, etc.

This demonstrates the leader's own commitment to the change process and his or her desire to involve others. This is a powerful tool as the following saying illustrates:

"Tell me and I'll forget;
Show me and I'll remember;
Involve me and I'll learn."

Another powerful tool is the use of benchmarks, internally and externally. Internally, by rewarding success; and externally, by demonstrating how other leaders and their organizations excel.

Leaders must find the *pearls* within their organizations and groom them for leadership. Leaders must also be willing to find those parts of the organization where *lions are being led by donkeys*! They should move the donkeys into donkey-positions. When you are leading what today is rapid change, you do not have the time or the ability to turn donkeys into lions.

INSTITUTIONALIZE THE CHANGE

"If it does not stick, it has not changed." This phase is of critical importance. Change, by its very nature, is disruptive – it dramatically alters the landscape of the organization; how work is done; and in the process, how people interact and communicate with each other throughout the organization. It is important to know that the change becomes embedded in the bloodstream of the organization when it becomes *business as usual* – that is, when the new behaviors become common individual and organizational practice. Thus, institutionalizing change is about making the new behaviors, processes, and procedures permanent.

The first step is to make a clear demonstration to the people of the effects of the changes in behaviors, processes, and procedures. Thus the leader would enable his people to visualize the cause and effect picture.

The second step is to invest sufficient time to ensure that the current leaders and leaders-in-training personify the new organizational approach and thinking. If this does not happen, there is the danger that poor leadership could undo years of excellent work.

The third step is for leaders to work to ensure that the shared philosophies, attitudes, expectations and norms that held the organization together were rigorously addressed – otherwise there is the threat of old habits creeping back.

The fourth step is to ensure that the *culture* of the organization is shaped and molded through continuous reinforcement and a goal-focused measurement system.

CONCLUSION

Leaders must balance a number of tensions. These include people and performance; the short and long term; sustaining current performance and growing for the future; finding the right balance between building better and building faster (remember the story of the three little pigs!). Whilst cost cutting skills (trimming off the lard) are important, leaders of change need to be able to spot and take new business opportunities. They need to constantly re-visit the strategy; re-jig the strategy if necessary; and keep their eyes on the performance indicators.

Leaders of change should beware of two pitfalls I have observed on change projects.

» The spirit of unconscious collusion.

This is when the change leader spews forth rhetoric and cannot translate words into action. His or her attitudes and beliefs do not match the vision he or she is espousing, and the leader mirrors the disbelief and the lethargy of the employees by reinforcing destructive patters of behavior. This kind of leader cannot artic- ulate the vision because he or she does not fully understand it. So, the followers rebel because they cannot see the moon in the darkest night – they do not have a story, so they weave their own based on their reading of the leader's walk. Since the leader cannot articulate the vision, they cannot see it; because they cannot see it, they cannot believe it. As they cannot believe it, they cannot will themselves into being it. Consequently, they cannot buy it and they cannot be it. Hence, the vision fails and the change initiative crumbles.

Also, instead of learning from past mistakes some leaders make the mistake of practicing what I call Constipation Management.

» Constipation Management.

"If it does not work, try harder." Since they see each problem as a nail, their only tool is a hammer, and try as they may, it still does not work. Rosabeth Moss Kanter stresses that "change- adept organizations" must continually replenish their stock of innovative ideas and "cannot afford to rest on the last great concept."

The role of the change leader has changed and become more complex, and definitely more critical to the organization's success. Leaders of change must:

» ensure that high performance levels are achieved and sustained;
» handle complexity and ambiguity; enjoy leading the change process;
» ensure that the organization, and its processes, are constantly evaluated and developed to deliver the vision, the strategy and performance; and
» ensure that the people within the company are motivated, empowered, developed, and rewarded to produce outstanding results.

It may seem that this is calling for leaders to be supermen or superwomen, and one may be right to assume so. It takes a lot of energy and will-power to lead any kind of fundamental change: leaders are asked to come up with the vision, develop the change plan, carry all the people with them, model the desired beliefs and behavior, motivate people, battle with and overcome resistance to change, and to recruit and develop change champions – whilst at the same time trying to keep the business afloat!

Unless you still believe in the "Incredible Hulk," you will conclude with me that it takes more than one man to guarantee the success of any change initiative, great or small.

In conclusion, the challenge for leaders in the present and in the future is to move themselves and their organizations towards the agile, adaptive, flexible, intelligent and spontaneous organization.

Search we must and each person must set out to cross his or her bridge. The important thing is to begin. However, you can stay at home, safe in the familiar illusion of certainty. Do not set out without realizing that the way is not without danger. Everything good is costly, and the development of the personality is one of the most costly of all things. It will cost you your innocence, your illusions, your certainty.

So, I leave you with these words, "my scars are well-earned and cannot be hid, so do what I learned, not what I did."

NOTES

1 Dess, G.G., Picken, J.C. & Lyon, D.W. (1998) "Transformational leadership: lessons from U.S. experience." *Long Range Planning, International Journal of Strategic Management*, The Strategic Planning Society, **31**(5) (October).
2 Schon, D. (1971) *Beyond the Stable State*. Hutchinson, London.
3 Sharman, C. (1997) "Looking for tomorrow's leaders." *Management Today*, August.

Frequently Asked Questions (FAQs)

Q1: What does "leadership" mean today?

A: See Chapters 1 and 2.

Q2: What are the main issues faced by leaders in the twenty-first century?

A: See Chapter 2.

Q3: How does a leader develop an "e" culture and optimize the use of the Net?

A: See Chapter 4.

Q4: How do leaders go about creating and managing a global business? What are the pitfalls to watch out for?

A: See Chapter 5.

Q5: What is the new thinking on leadership and change?

A: See Chapters 2 and 6.

Q6: What are the impacts of the new sciences (complexity), uncertainty and speed? How does a leader manage complexity?

A: See Chapters 2, 6 and 10.

Q7: How have leading organizations and leaders responded to managing change (the success stories)?

A: See Chapter 7.

Q8: How can a leader manage resistance to change? How does a leader get '*buy-in*'?

A: See Chapter 10.

Q9: What are the tips for leading and institutionalizing change? What kinds of leaders will succeed?

A: See Chapter 10.

Q10: What if the culture of the organization threatens the change and it is difficult to uproot embedded patterns of destructive or non-progressive organizational beliefs and behaviors?

A: See Chapters 6, 7 and 10.

Acknowledgments

This book is dedicated to my daughter, Naomi. Thank you for your patience and understanding whilst I have been writing the book.

As with any list of thanks, it is easier to know where to start than it is to know where to end – but I would like to mention the following: Dr Ian McGill, Richard Lewis, Mark Long, Pete Floyd, Folu Akin-Taylor, Tina Bamwo, Yinka Badejo, Vinay Khosla, Bernadette Kimona, Bernadette Olagunju, Ian McGowan, Ash Halim, Professor Patrick Pietroni, Wole Ajayi, and Dr Dow Smith. Thank you all for all your support and encouragement. Thank you to all the dedicated people at Capstone Publishing, in particular, Mark Allin. Finally, I thank God for being my inspiration.

Although I have endeavoured to acknowledge many of my sources, it is likely that I may have missed some – I apologize for any oversights in this respect.

In memory of Deborah Tempest, a *spectacular, shooting star*.

About the Author

Olu works as an Organizational and Human Performance Consultant and she specializes in organizational change management and business coaching.

She is a part-time lecturer in Organizational Learning and Development on a Master's Degree course at the University of Kent in Canterbury.

She is also a life coach and has developed continuous professional development processes and leadership programs for various organizations in different sectors.

She is very committed to the voluntary sector and she works as a mentor and regional assessor for the Prince's Trust. She is currently developing a Leadership Skills Development Program for young people.

Index